$23.50

5 6021 00013 5438

D1001599

Theft by
Employees

Theft by Employees

Richard C. Hollinger
University of Florida

John P. Clark
University of Minnesota

LexingtonBooks
D.C. Heath and Company
Lexington, Massachusetts
Toronto

Library of Congress Cataloging in Publication Data

Hollinger, Richard C.
    Theft by employees.

    Includes index.
    1. Employee theft. I. Clark, John P. II. Title.
HF5549.5.E43H64   1983   658.4′73   82-48028
ISBN 0-669-05887-4

Copyright © 1983 by D.C. Heath and Company

Second printing, March 1985

Published simultaneously in Canada

Printed in the United States of America

International Standard Book Number: 0-669-05887-4

Library of Congress Catalog Card Number: 82-48028

To those from whom we have stolen time:

Candy and Lindsay Hollinger
and
Shirley, Mary, David, and Timothy Clark

Contents

Contents ix

Figures and Tables

Preface

Although employee theft has been the subject of a number of articles and a handful of books, readers will find this book to be a rather different perspective to this interesting and perplexing topic. The difference in approaches is attributable to the fact that most other writers on this subject have been professionals in the field of private or industrial security. Sociologists view the phenomenon of employee theft not from a law-enforcement perspective but as a set of behaviors to be explained via the various structures and processes operating in the work milieu. From this sociological perspective, then, our primary objective is to identify those factors that may help us to understand theft and other deviant acts by employees. We firmly believe that only through a more empirically based understanding of this subject can corporate management ever hope to respond appropriately to this problem.

This book represents an example of how the academic and business communities can cooperate to achieve mutually beneficial goals that neither community could reach alone. During the course of the research process we encountered a persistent minority of skeptics who maintained that either research on such a sensitive topic could not be done or, if completed, that nothing new will be learned. We hope that this book is convincing evidence disproving both of these pessimistic assertions. Further, we hope that the successful completion of this cooperative effort will increase the receptivity of corporate executives in the future when they are approached to participate in similar research ventures. Only in this way can our present state of knowledge on subjects like this be improved systematically.

Acknowledgments

The three-year pursuit of research objectives involving a federal agency (in the process of being reorganized), a large state university, a nonprofit business-education organization, various professional associations, forty-seven business corporations in three major U.S. cities, almost 10,000 of their employees, close to 250 of their top executives, and over thirty labor unions and employee associations is in itself a notable monument to the virtues of goodwill, patience, trust, and appreciation for systematic scientific inquiry.

In such a complex enterprise, the success of the effort depends largely upon the expertise of the research team. Without the superior effort exhibited by the following people, this project could not have been completed: Philip Cooper (data manager and analyst); Peter Parilla (research associate and principal author of chapter 8); Robbie Friedmann, Gerry Larson, Jerry Parker, Joe Raiche, Brad Richardson, Phil Smith-Cunnien, Deborah Staal, and David Zander (research assistants); Crystal Gandrud, Janice Manis, and Lois Norem (secretaries); Holly Norman and Carla Ade (typists); and Candy Hollinger (graphics).

We also wish to recognize the substantial contribution of our colleague, Mr. Leonard Smith of the American Management Association, who as our subcontractor during the crucial first phase of the research helped immeasurably to plan the project and to facilitate our access to the business community. During this period we also benefited greatly from the goodwill of Mr. Gordon Williams of the National Retail Merchants Association, Mr. Richard Hersch of the National Mass Retailing Institute, and the Central Minnesota Chapter of the American Society for Industrial Security.

Various of our academic colleagues from around the country also helped to facilitate and guide our work. Most important, Professors Howard Aldrich, Richard Hall, Charles Hulin, and Ezra Krendall served on our advisory committee. Further, Professors Richard Hawkins and Mark Lefton provided local liaison in Dallas-Fort Worth and Cleveland, respectively. Professors Al Reiss and Michael Barrett helped to critique our data-collection procedures. Finally, we wish to recognize the contribution made by Dr. Sidney Epstein and Dr. Fred Heinzelmann, our project monitors at the National Institute of Justice, which provided the financial support for this research effort.

We are forever grateful to the thousands of employees who confidentially provided sometimes very sensitive information for our analysis. Their personal identities and those of their corporate employers obviously must remain anonymous. We hope their contribution will be of significant benefit to all those involved in both scholarly and policymaking pursuits.

This research project was supported by grant numbers 78-NI-AX-0014 and 79-NI-AX-0090, awarded to the Department of Sociology, University of Minnesota, by the National Institute of Justice, U.S. Department of Justice, under the Omnibus Crime Control and Safe Streets Act of 1968, as amended. Points of view or opinions stated in this book are those of the authors and do not necessarily represent the official position or policies of the U.S. Department of Justice.

Theft by
Employees

1 Employee Theft

The study of crime traditionally has attempted to understand the minority of society's members whose behavior exceeds the limit of the criminal law. Historically, those interested in studying criminality have focused their primary attention on certain types of crime, ignoring others. The most visible locus of both criminal and scholarly activity has been *street crime*. This focus is no doubt attributable to the fact that many of society's more-frightening and dramatic crimes such as murder, assault, robbery, and rape often take place in city streets or other public places. Not surprising, the profile of the typical offender has indicated disproportionately greater criminal involvement by members of the lower classes, youths, minorities, and other persons marginal to basic social institutions. As Alexander Liazos has colorfully phrased it, the history of criminology has concentrated almost exclusively on the activities of "nuts, sluts and preverts [*sic*],"[1] virtually ignoring the criminality of society's middle and upper classes.[2]

A notable exception to this trend is exemplified in the work of Edwin Sutherland. As a result of his classic study of criminal behavior by corporations, the discipline of criminology and the public at large began to recognize the offenses committed by individuals usually perceived to be law abiding, a phenomenon that Sutherland called white-collar crime.[3] The term *white-collar crime* has come to represent a wide range of socially injurious behavior of individuals and corporations perpetrated during the course of day-to-day occupational and organizational activity.[4] While Sutherland's 1939 challenge for criminology to abandon its lower-class-linked theories of criminal behavior received wide acclaim, only quite recently have criminologists taken the challenge seriously by examining alternative settings of criminal behavior.

Crime in the Work Place

One very important and long ignored locus of criminal activity has been the work place. Consistent with criminology's long held obsession with the deviance of the lower classes, for many years crime has been perceived as the almost exclusive activity of the nonworking or unemployed members of the population. Despite the fact that most individuals spend a major portion of their adult lives at their jobs, we have either overlooked criminal activity that occurs in the work place or have referred to it with noncriminal labels such as "the fiddle," "pilferage," "fringes," or "just business."[5]

As theorists have begun to look at the work place as an environment of possible criminal activity, they have found it useful to make the distinction between crimes by business (that is, corporate crime) and crimes against business by employees (that is, occupational crime).[6] For example, on the subject of crimes by business, Clinard and his associates recently have documented the pervasive criminal careers of some of the largest and most respected *Fortune* 500 corporations in the United States.[7] While this is an important dimension of the phenomenon of work-place crime, instead, the focus of this book is concentrated on those acts committed against the business organization—more specifically, the theft of organizational assets by employees within the work place.

Employee Theft

By *employee theft*, we specifically mean the unauthorized taking, control, or transfer of money and/or property of the formal work organization that is perpetrated by an employee during the course of occupational activity.[8] The methods by which employees victimize the property of their employers are both profuse in number and sometimes elaborate in design. Employee theft may take the form of borrowing money from a cash register; taking merchandise, supplies, or tools home in handbags and lunch boxes; or more- complicated manipulations of organizational assets (more recently by computer) for personal benefit.

Approximations of the impact of employee theft upon economic activity are at best educated guesses given the difficulty in measuring the phenomenon accurately. Nevertheless, to satisfy the demand of the business community to know how much there is, the American Management Associations (AMA) in 1975 collected data in order to estimate the total cost of crimes against business.[9] As we can see in figure 1-1, the total dollar impact of nonviolent crimes against business is estimated by the AMA to be in excess of $40 billion a year.[10] Of these many types of victimizations, the theft of company property by employees is estimated to be the single most significant dollar-impact offense category of these eleven crimes committed against business.[11]

Experts in various industries regularly cite their own figures, attributing employee theft as either a relatively minor problem or the single most important problem of U.S. business. This glaring discrepancy no doubt is due to the fact that no one really knows for sure the scope of employee theft. For example, in order to calculate the level of theft by employees, retailers work from their inventory-shrinkage (or shortage) statistics, which represent

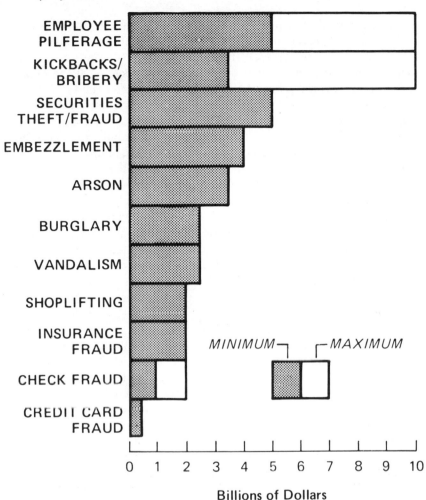

Adapted with permission from American Management Associations, 1977.

Figure 1-1. Estimates of Losses Due to Nonviolent Crimes against Business, 1975

the inventory deficit in dollars that cannot be accounted for after sales reductions and remaining unsold stock have been subtracted from initial inventories. However, even if one can arrive at an exact inventory-shrinkage figure (usually expressed as a percentage of gross sales), the proportion of the figure that is attributable solely to employee theft remains intertwined with other confounding sources of loss. Factors such as clerical and billing errors, conventional theft, and shoplifing, equally as difficult to measure, also contribute to the total inventory-shrinkage level. Most inventory-control and loss-prevention experts privately will admit that separating out the effects of employee theft from these other alternative sources of shrinkage has been virtually an impossible task because of the great difficulties involved in assessing the source of a loss after the fact.

Although there may be difficulties in determining the amount of employee theft, there appears to be little debate as to who pays the cost of such crime. When profits are adversely affected, small firms with limited liquid capital are often forced out of business. The Chamber of Commerce reports that over 30 percent of all business failures in a given year may be attributable to significant employee-theft problems.[12] Larger companies that temporarily can absorb theft losses eventually must pass the cost along to insurance companies, consumers, and the taxpayer (that is, as an uninsured-business-loss deduction). The economic impact of employee theft and other crimes against business is most immediately reflected in terms of higher prices in the marketplace. An estimate made five years ago placed the added price of employee theft and pilferage at 12 cents out every dollar spent.[13] No doubt this figure is substantially higher today because of inflation.

Despite these impressive figures, the bottom line for employee theft and other crimes against business cannot be measured solely in terms of dollars and cents. The social impact, not only to those involved but also to fellow workers and the organization, must be calculated into the total as well.

The negative consequences to the individual employee detected for theft involvement can be rather significant. Although many companies admit that they detect a small minority of the total number of employees who have stolen from the firm, when they do officially apprehend someone, the most common corporate reaction is to terminate the offending worker immediately. The financial implications and emotional stress brought about by immediate job loss are obvious. Further, what is not often understood by the terminated worker is the fact that many companies informally share names of dismissed employees, thereby preventing future employment with other participating firms in that specific industry or geographical area.[14]

To the knowledgeable employee who is not personally involved, theft by fellow workers may create social barriers that impede the development of co-worker trust. These communication and interaction barriers, between those who are involved in theft and those who are not, negatively affect most aspects of the employment experience.

Some firms react to detected or imagined theft with draconian security devices designed to deter future employee theft.[15] Many employees who are forced to work in these security-intensive work environments often report that they feel untrusted by their employers—probably an accurate conclusion.[16] Other firms take the ostrich approach by ignoring the problem, hoping that it will go away before the company is negatively affected.[17] Tacitly ignoring the occurrence of theft no doubt sends the signal to the entire work force that the firm does not really care about its property or the level of employee integrity. In sum, when we take into consideration the incalculable social costs like those mentioned, the grand total paid for theft in the work place is no doubt grossly underestimated by the available financial estimates.

Given the rather insurmountable difficulties in assessing the extent of employee theft by utilizing dollar-loss estimates, other sources of data might be more illustrative of theft's prevalence. The principal alternative estimation strategy relies on determining the percentage or proportion of the work force involved in employee theft. As we found with the financial-loss estimates, available data on the prevalence of employee theft range from educated guesses by experts in the private-security industry to a handful of empirical research efforts.

The best known statistics on employee involvement in theft come from the accumulated wisdom of acknowledged experts in the area of private and industrial security. During their years of investigations within all types and sizes of firms, many of the nation's foremost security consultants have made generalized conclusions regarding the percentage of employees involved in theft. For example, Mark Lipman, president of a major industrial-security organization and an experienced private investigator, believes that approximately one-half of all employees steal to some degree, 25 percent of whom take important items, while 8 percent steal in volume.[18] Our review of the security literature published since 1973 suggests some degree of consensus on these percentages. However, this apparent consensus may be attributable to the fact that Lipman's personal estimates have been repeated often by others without citation and have thus begun to take on the reputation of proven fact.[19]

Other estimates of the extent of employee-theft involvement abound, ranging widely from 9 percent[20] to 75 percent[21]—all depending on the source of the estimate. The reason there is so much diversity in these figures is no doubt due to the fact that very little empirical data are available upon which to estimate reliably the prevalence of employee theft.

The few empirically supported studies on the incidence of employee theft also yield statistics that vary widely. For example, Ronald Schmidt reports that 76 percent of the workers who received a polygraph examination admitted involvement in employee theft.[22] Of the ninety-eight retail employees nonrandomly interviewed by Ronald Tatham, 50 percent admitted to "taking merchandise from their place of employment without paying for it."[23] Philip Ash reports that both polygraph examinations and pre-employment screening tests reject an average of 30-32 percent of the applicants—many of whom are excluded after admitting to prior theft behavior.[24] Finally, Hollinger found (in a study that served as a pilot to this book) that 28 percent of a random sample of 339 midwestern retail employees admitted taking either money or property from their employers.[25]

Trying to draw firm conclusions from such a small number of self-report studies is quite difficult. Perhaps the most we can say is that theft by employees is a significant and pervasive part of the work experience with between one-half and one-quarter of the typical work force involved in taking company money or property sometime during their employment. The reader should note, however, that further complicating this conclusion is the finding that employee theft exhibits a bimodal distribution;[26] that is, a very small number of employees take large amounts while the vast majority of those involved in theft take relatively small amounts—a pattern that parallels the distribution of deviance reported in many other self-reported studies.[27]

Understanding Employee Theft

Thus far we have recognized that employee theft is a social and economic problem of some significance. However, continuing to dwell solely upon the dollar-impact or prevalence issue can be a dead end given the more-important unanswered questions. Developing a theoretical understanding and explanation of employee theft not only is the primary focus of the remainder of this chapter but also is the principal objective of this book.

Arriving at some consensus as to the causes of employee theft has been an elusive goal of many researchers in the disciplines of sociology, criminology, psychology, anthropology, and industrial security. As with almost any complex behavioral phenomenon, a cursory review of the scholarly literature clearly demonstrates the lack of agreement among those who are supposed to be experts on employee theft. Untested and partially tested hypotheses abound. In the last five years alone, two exhaustive literature reviews clearly have illustrated the plethora of theoretical paradigms available to understand employee theft.[28] Our purpose is not only to organize the theory that promises to be most beneficial in understanding this phenomenon but also to test empirically many of the related hypotheses that have been suggested.

The articles that make an attempt to understand employee theft offer many varied explanatory themes. From this extensive body of literature we have been able to identify five separate but interrelated sets of hypotheses explaining employee theft. They include a broad range of variables including economic, individual personal, and organizational influences.[29]

External Economic Pressures

The most frequently observed explanatory theme regarding employee theft is based on external economic pressures. The assumption commonly expressed is that employees who steal from the company have gotten themselves into an "unshareable problem,"[30] usually involving either "gin, girls or gambling" or "babes, booze and bookies."[31] Employees choose taking things from their employers as a method to acquire the necessary resources to extricate themselves from various financial dilemmas. While this theory has not been studied systematically (with the exception of Cressey's study of embezzlement), it is a pervasive explanation found most frequently in the industrial-security literature.[32] This explanation is very popular with those who believe that the same explanations used to predict conventional (or street) criminality also apply to employee theft; that is, it is theorized that when economic pressures become great,[33] people may turn to illegitimate means to achieve socially acceptable goals.[34] Typically left unexplicated are the connections between the nature of the economic needs and the manner in which the stolen materials satisfy those needs.

Youth and Work

Another commonly expressed theory of employee theft focuses on the honesty and integrity of younger U.S. workers. More specifically, the argument is made that contemporary employees (especially the very young) are not as hard working or honest as those of past generations. Those who advocate this theory suggest that this alleged "epidemic of moral laxity" among the younger members of the work force is causally related to employee theft.[35] When one examines the circumstantial evidence for this theory, the results at first glance are surprisingly supportive. Two studies of apprehended retail-employee thieves conducted in the past twelve years suggest disproportionately greater theft involvement among younger and newly hired employees.[36] The retail industry's heightened concern about these findings is attributable in large part to the increasingly greater reliance placed upon the younger high-school and college-age employee in order to meet consumer demand for longer store hours. The specific question that must be answered is whether younger employees are more involved in theft than their older co-workers. If they are, is their involvement attributable to a generational morality difference, or is it simply a by-product of the type of work that is required of younger employees?

Opportunity

Our third identifiable theory is a more-pessimistic corollary to the two explanatory models discussed previously. Many persons, particularly those with years of experience in the industrial-security profession, have come to the conclusion that every employee can be tempted to steal from his employer.[37] This theory is based upon the assumption that everyone is basically greedy and dishonest by nature, with larcenous tendencies lurking only barely beneath the surface. For those who advocate this theory of employee theft, the key to understanding this phenomenon is in knowing the relative levels of opportunity the employee has to steal.[38] Thus, with high opportunity will come correspondingly high levels of employee theft, and vice versa. Although there is an obvious danger in this theory being tautological (that is, people steal because they can steal), reducing employee theft under this model consists of constraining the opportunity for theft in the work place—in short, bolting everything down.

Job Dissatisfaction

After reviewing the available literature that purports to explain employee theft, Dwight Merriam concludes that job dissatisfaction among members of the work force is "perhaps the most important and least understood cause of employee theft."[39] Until recently, the hypothesis that conditions within the work place may exacerbate or even be the primary cause of theft has not been accepted as a palatable explanatory paradigm.[40] While preceding theoretical models have looked to the employee's background or other external conditions for an explanation of theft behavior, this theory proposes that the victimized organization may play a part in determining the level of theft behavior of its own employees by influencing their perceived level of dissatisfaction with their jobs.[41]

Social Control

The fifth and final explanatory theme we have been able to identify is a social-control theory of employee theft. Again, as with job dissatisfaction, the primary explanatory variables in this theory come from within the work place. Social-control theory suggests that theft persists due to the broadly shared informal and formal social structure that has developed over time. Here we are interested in the normative sanctions (both positive and negative) that determine and regulate the tolerable limits of deviant behavior in the work setting. A number of recent qualitative studies document the role that the work group's norms play in controlling theft by employees.[42] In addition, there is evidence of a relationship between supervisory/management personnel and employees in constraining or encouraging theft behavior.[43] Although not yet empirically tested, from these studies it becomes clear that the phenomenon of employee theft also can be viewed from a "deterrence doctrine" perspective.[44] This deterrence model assumes that deviant work-place behavior may be affected by the threat of negative social sanction, from either the organization itself or the criminal law. Specifically, theorists using the deterrence doctrine to explain law-violative behavior suggest that three critical variables—certainty, severity, and celerity of punishment—are important to understanding the deterrent effect that a social control will have on behavior.[45] Recent consensus of empirical research has concluded that of these three factors, certainty of punishment has been shown to be more salient in shaping behavior than either severity or celerity of punishment.[46] In the employment setting we would hypothesize, then, that employees who perceive the sanction threat of detection and punishment to be nonexistent or minimal will more likely be involved in various types of employee theft.

Other theories of employee theft that have not been mentioned may exist, but these are the five most commonly articulated hypotheses. The reader should be aware, however, that these differing theories are probably not mutually exclusive, but they each may help to explain some aspect or category of theft among this rather diverse group of deviant work-place behaviors.

Employee Deviance

Although our expressed topic of interest is employee theft, it is evident that the taking of company property and money is not the only type of deviance possible by employees that is detrimental to the interests of the work organization and to their own work status. In fact, a review of the literature in the sociology of work over the past few decades suggests that counterproductive behavior, not theft, may be the more-pervasive form of rule-breaking behavior committed by employees. When we consider the various documented forms of counterproductive employee behavior such as the unauthorized use of time-saving tools,[47] goldbricking,[48] informal co-worker interaction,[49] wildcat strikes,[50] or industrial sabotage,[51] the total range of deviance possible in the work place broadens significantly. From a theoretical standpoint, then, the more-inclusive phenomenon under study might more accurately be labeled *employee deviance* with two primary subcategories—acts by employees against the property of the organization and the violations of the norms regulating acceptable levels of production.[52]

Since we cannot theoretically divorce deviant acts against the property of the organization (that is, employee theft) from the more-prevalent and frequently less-serious instances of production deviance, we strived to obtain information regarding both subcategories of employee deviance throughout our research. Therefore, in the following chapters we consider the broader concept, employee deviance, operationalized in terms of its two most common manifestations, property and production deviance. Our principal emphasis remains focused on property deviance, or employee theft. (The reader should note that we refer to property deviance and employee theft interchangeably in subsequent chapters.) However, when appropriate, we also examine the correlates of production deviance (or counterproductive behavior) as well. By broadening our horizon of interest in this way, we hope to understand better work-place theft, particularly its relationship to the more-prevalent nonproperty manifestations of employee deviance.

Research Objectives

The principal objective of this book is to develop information upon which to base a comprehensive understanding of work-place theft and related deviant behaviors. Five specific questions guide the study. First, how much employee theft and other kinds of work-place deviance is occurring in the typical business organization? Second, under what circumstances (both individual and organizational) would these behaviors be most likely to occur? Third, what might be the most effective steps that management and labor could take to reduce the prevalence of employee theft and counterproductive behavior in their organizations? Fourth, do certain characteristics of communities in which work organizations are located affect rates of deviance within the work place? Finally, but most important, can research on such a sensitive topic be conducted successfully? This book is physical evidence in answer to the fifth question. The remainder of this book concerns itself with providing answers to the remaining questions.

Notes

1. A. Liazos, "The Poverty of the Sociology of Deviance: Nuts, Sluts, and 'Preverts'," *Social Problems* 20 (1972):103-120.

2. A. Thio, "Class Bias in the Sociology of Deviance," *American Sociologist* 8 (1973):1-12; and S. Box and J. Ford, "The Facts Don't Fit: On the Relationship between Social Class and Criminal Behavior," *Sociological Inquiry* 19 (1971):31-52.

3. Edwin H. Sutherland, "White-Collar Criminality," *American Sociological Review* 5 (1940):1-12.

4. Edwin H. Sutherland, *White Collar Crime* (New York: Holt, Rinehart & Winston, 1949).

5. J. Ditton, "Perks, Pilferage, and the Fiddle: The Historical Structure of Invisible Wages," *Theory and Society* 4 (1977):39-71.

6. Marshall B. Clinard and Richard Quinney, *Criminal Behavior Systems: A Typology*, 2d ed. (New York: Holt, Rinehart & Winston, 1973), pp. 187-223.

7. Marshall B. Clinard et al., *Illegal Corporate Behavior* (Washington, D.C.: Government Printing Office, 1979).

8. D. Merriam, "Employee Theft," *Criminal Justice Abstracts* 9 (1977):380-386; and G. Robin, "White Collar Crime and Employee Theft," *Crime and Delinquency* 20 (1974):251-262.

9. American Management Associations, "Summary Overview of the 'State of the Art' Regarding Information Gathering Techniques and Level of Knowledge in Three Areas Concerning Crimes against Business" Draft report (Washington, D.C.: National Institute of Law Enforcement and Criminal Justice, Law Enforcement Assistance Administration, March 1977), pp. 17-19.

10. Ibid.

11. Ibid.

12. Chamber of Commerce of the United States, *A Handbook of White Collar Crime* (Washington, D.C., 1974), p. 4.

13. "Crime in Business: Stop Employee Theft, It's Money Down the Drain," *Canadian Business* 49 (1976):12, 14, 16.

14. Stores' Mutual Protective Association, Third Annual Security Seminar, New York, 16 April 1980).

15. "Space Age Devices to Outwit Thieves," *U.S. News & World Report* 75 (2 July 1973):75-76.

16. "Who's Doing the Stealing?" *Management Review* 61 (May 1972):34-35; and G.M. Rekstad, "Industrial TV: The Picture Clears," *Factory* 7 (1974):25-33.

17. "Crime in Business," *Canadian Business*.

18. Mark Lipman, *Stealing: How America's Employees Are Stealing Their Companies Blind* (New York: Harper's Magazine Press, 1973).

19. A. Broy. "The $40 Billion Rip Off," *Finance Magazine* 92 (November 1974):42-45; and Chamber of Commerce of the United States, *Handbook of White Collar Crime*.

20. "A $40-Billion Crime Wave Swamps American Business: Firms of All Sizes Are Being Drained of Cash and Merchandise by Professional Thieves and Their Own Workers," *U.S. News & World Report* 82 (21 February 1977):47-48.

21. L. Zeitlin, "A Little Larceny Can Do a Lot for Employee Morale," *Psychology Today* 5 (1971):22, 24, 26, 64.

22. R.R. Schmidt, "Executive Dishonesty: Misuse of Authority for Personal Gain," in *Internal Theft: Investigation and Control*, ed. Sheryl Leininger (Los Angeles: Security World Publishing Co., 1975), pp. 69-81.

23. R.L. Tatham, "Employee's Views on Theft in Retailing," *Journal of Retailing* (Fall 1974), pp. 49-55.

24. P. Ash, "Screening Employment Applications for Attitudes toward Theft," *Journal of Applied Psychology* 55 (1971):161-164.

25. Richard C. Hollinger, *Employee Deviance: Acts against the Formal Work Organization* (Ann Arbor, Mich.: University Microfilm, 1979).

26. Ibid.

27. Roger Hood and Richard Sparks, *Key Issues in Criminology* (New York: McGraw-Hill, 1970), pp. 46-79.

28. Merriam, "Employee Theft"; and D.L. Altheide et al., "The Social Meanings of Employee Theft," in *Crime at the Top*, eds. John M. Johnson and Jack D. Douglas (Philadelphia: Lippincott, 1978), pp. 90-124.

29. Merriam, "Employee Theft."

30. Donald Cressey, *Other People's Money: A Study in the Social Psychology of Embezzlement* (Belmont, Calif.: Wadsworth, 1953).

31. J.S. Seidman, "Business Frauds: Their Perpetration, Detection, and Redress, Part 1," *National Public Accountant* 10 (August 1965):16-18.

32. W.E. Backman, "Pilferage, Payola and Protection," *Office Executive* 36 (1961):26-27.

33. C.A. Nekvasil, "As Paychecks Shrink, Industry Theft Problems Grow," *Industry Week* 82 (1974):11-12.

34. R.K. Merton, "Social Structure and Anomie," *American Sociological Review* 3 (1938):672-682.

35. Merriam, "Employee Theft."

36. G. Robin, "Employees as Offenders," *Journal of Research on Crime and Delinquency* 6 (1969):17-33; and Alice Pickett Franklin, *Internal Theft in a Retail Organization: A Case Study* (Ann Arbor, Mich.: University Microfilms, 1975).

37. S.D. Astor, "Who's Doing the Stealing?" *Management Review* 61 (1972):34-35.

38. C.F. Hemphill, Jr., "Cutting Pilferage, Petty Cash Losses," *Administrative Management* 30 (February 1969):40, 42, 44.

39. Merriam, "Employee Theft," p. 395.

40. D.C. Jones, "Employee Theft in Organizations," *Society for the Advancement of Management* 37 (1972):59-63; and Zeitlin, "A Little Larceny."

41. M.C. Dillon, "Why Should Anyone Refrain from Stealing?" *Ethics* 83 (1973):338-340; T.W. Mangione and R.P. Quinn, "Job Satisfaction, Counter-Productive Behavior, and Drug Use at Work," *Journal of Applied Psychology* 11 (1975):114-116; Richard Quinney, *Class, State and Crime: On the Theory and Practice of Criminal Justice* (New York: David McKay, 1977), pp. 54-55; Ditton, "Perks, Pilferage, and the Fiddle"; and R.C. Hollinger and J.P. Clark, "Employee Deviance: A Response to the Perceived Quality of the Work Experience," *Work and Occupations* 9 (1982): 97-114.

42. D. Horning, "Blue Collar Theft: Conceptions of Property, Attitudes toward Pilfering, and Work Group Norms in a Modern Industrial Plant," in *Crimes against Bureaucracy*, eds. Erwin O. Smigel and H. Laurence Ross (New York: Van Nostrand Reinhold, 1970), pp. 46-64; G. Mars, "Chance, Punters, and the Fiddle: Institutionalized Pilferage in a Hotel Dining Room," in *The Sociology of the Workplace*, ed. M. Warner (New York: Halsted Press, 1973), pp. 200-210; and G. Mars, "Dock Pilferage: A Case Study in Occupational Theft," in *Deviance and Control*, eds. Paul Rock and Mary McIntosh (London: Tavistock, 1974), pp. 209-228.

43. Alvin W. Gouldner, *Wildcat Strike: A Study in Worker-Management Relationships* (New York: Harper & Row, 1954; J. Bensman and I. Gerver, "Crime and Punishment in the Factory: The Function of Deviancy in Maintaining the Social System," *American Sociological Review* 28 (1963):588-598; and Norman Jaspan, *Mind Your Own Business* (Englewood Cliffs, N.J.: Prentice-Hall, 1974).

44. Jack P. Gibbs, *Crime, Punishment, and Deterrence* (New York: Elsevier, 1975).

45. C.R. Tittle and C.H. Logan, "Sanctions and Deviance: Evidence and Remaining Questions," *Law and Society Review* 7 (1973):371-392.

46. G.F. Jensen et al., "Perceived Risk of Punishment and Self-Reported Delinquency," *Social Forces* 57 (1978):57-78; and Charles R. Tittle, *Sanctions and Social Deviance: The Question of Deterrence* (New York: Praeger, 1980), pp. 7-12.

47. Bensman and Gerver, "Crime and Punishment."

48. D.F. Roy, "Quota Restrictions and Goldbricking in a Machine Shop," *American Journal of Sociology* 57 (1952):427-442.

49. D.F. Roy, "Banana Time: Job Satisfaction and Informal Interaction," *Human Organization* 18 (1959):158-168.

50. Gouldner, *Wildcat Strike*.

51. Laurie Taylor and Paul Walton, "Industrial Sabotage: Motives and Meanings," in *Images of Deviance*, ed. S. Cohen (London: Penguin, 1971), pp. 219-245.

52. Hollinger, *Employee Deviance*.

2 Research Methodology

The most significant limitation of the available studies on property and production deviance by employees has been the absence of a representative set of data from which to draw reliable generalizations. Conclusions about employee theft that are based upon an individual's personal observations or a single company's inventory-shrinkage statistics cannot contribute substantially to a comprehensive understanding of this phenomenon. Even the qualitative case studies that in the past have yielded such colorful anecdotal findings about specific instances of documented property and production employee deviance are grossly inadequate when answering questions concerning representativeness and generalizability. For this book to add significantly to our knowledge of employee deviance, a substantially different research methodology was required.

Our decision not to base this book on existing data sources was not made capriciously. Prior to proposing any new research methodologies, we first explored what was known currently about the prevalence of employee deviance, particularly property theft. Unfortunately, a review of the few available empirical studies, corporate data on theft, conversations with industrial-security experts, and our own exploratory research told us what we had already suspected—that no one really knows the scope and dimensions of the employee-theft phenomenon.[1] Even companies with sophisticated state-of-the-art inventory-control systems cannot determine accurately how much of their inventory shrinkage is attributable to theft by employees. Further, since no trade association, insurance company, or law-enforcement or other governmental agency has access to any data sources independent from the inexact estimates provided to them by private firms, it is impossible to study theft by utilizing secondary data sources. In sum, unless one wants to study apprehended workers, usually considered to be an extremely skewed subsample,[2,3] the only viable alternative was to develop an innovative data-collection effort not reliant upon existing information sources.

Sources of Data

In response to the prevailing paucity of information on this phenomenon, our research methodology includes three separate, but complementary, data sources: (1) a self-report questionnaire survey of employees, (2) interviews with organizational executives, and (3) face-to-face employee interviews.

Our preliminary research suggested that methodological techniques used in the past to study deviant behavior in other settings also might prove adaptable to measuring the deviant acts by employees against their employers.[4] Specifically, as the principal data-collection technique we utilized a self-report survey questionnaire. A random sample of employees from each of the participating companies anonymously provided data on personal and occupational characteristics, job satisfaction, perceptions of theft deterrents, and most important, their own personal involvement across a wide range of deviant behaviors in the work place, including theft of company property and money.

As a second major source of data, certain key management executives were interviewed personally to determine their organization's knowledge of and response to employee theft. This concerted effort to focus on the nature of the work organization arose out of our review of available research on this subject, signaling clearly that all organizations are not alike in their approach to employee theft. While some organizations seem to ignore the phenomenon, others take a resolute stance as exemplified in their formal policies and procedures.

Realizing that we did not have the time, expertise, or financial resources to evaluate exhaustively each organization on all aspects related to employee theft, the next best choice was selected. In each of the participating organizations, we personally interviewed the chief executive officer (or administrator), chief financial officer (and internal auditor, if possible), personnel manager, inventory-control manager, and loss-prevention or security director. Each provided us with information on the employee-theft phenomenon from his or her particular area of responsibility within the organization.

Finally, from its earliest planning stages, this book was designed to incorporate a face-to-face interview with typical employees from representative companies already surveyed by questionnaire and executive interview. This rich source of qualitative data was thought to be critical for a comprehensive understanding of the circumstances under which employees misuse property and production time within work organizations.

Over a period of several months near the end of the research project, extended structured conversations were held with employees from six organizations, two from each of the three industry sectors included in the study. These interviews were designed to elicit answers to questions that could not be discerned from the pages of a returned questionnaire booklet or from the opinions of a corporate executive. Through these face-to-face interviews, workers provided us with their unique insights on the processes, patterns, meanings, and perceptions of the complex factors impinging upon employees during their daily work routines. This final qualitative component thus complements the more-quantitative sources of data discussed earlier, yielding a truly multimethod approach to the central research problem.

Research Design

To collect data about the employee-deviance phenomenon both from individual employees and corporate executives, we designed a two-phase research methodology. During the first phase we limited our study to the organizations and the work force of one community in three differing industry sectors. The second phase was designed to replicate the research within two alternative communities in addition to conducting the qualitative face-to-face employee interviews.

Phase I

For Phase I, we implemented our research design in the Minneapolis-St. Paul Standard Metropolitan Statistical Area (SMSA). Our primary reason for selecting this metropolitan area was the established good relationship between the local business community and the University of Minnesota, under whose auspices the project was conducted. This relationship was important because, in order to obtain the desired information about employee theft, we would have to acquire the complete cooperation of a significant number of business organizations.

Upon initiation of the study, we recognized that industries vary widely by features relevant to emplyee theft, such as the characteristics of their work forces, their technologies, and the physical products they handle. On the one hand, we wished to incorporate the breadth of work-place variety, yet we also wanted to make our results as focused and industry specific as possible. Therefore, as a compromise, we chose to focus on the three most populous sectors of U.S. industry: retail, manufacturing, and service.

Specifically tailoring the study to represent the strengths of the Twin Cities' business community within these three sectors, we further narrowed our focus to retail merchandise corporations, electronics-manufacturing firms, and general hospitals. Since the decision to participate was made totally by the organization, we could not design a perfectly representative sample. Instead, our goal was to obtain the permission of approximately ten typical organizations in each of the three industries chosen. It was also important to our research interests that each of the organizations be large enough to permit the collection of the kinds of data required by our working hypotheses.

The entry procedure into organizations began with press releases about the project from the University of Minnesota and the AMA, our Phase I subcontractor. Subsequently, with the help of the Minneapolis and St. Paul Chambers of Commerce, executive officers from Twin Cities businesses were briefed on the study. Eventually, thirty-five organizations agreed to participate in Phase I: nine retailers, ten manufacturing firms, and sixteen hospitals.

Of the nine retail organizations in the first phase of the study, three operate full-line department stores that sell a wide variety of products including clothing, jewelry, furniture, and appliances. Two organizations operate discount stores that are essentially self-serve operations—that is, a customer enters a store through a single point of entry, selects merchandise, and takes it to a central checkout cashier. Three other companies operate specialty shops—that is, stores that concentrate on a single line of merchandise such as clothing or sporting goods. Also included in the retail-sector sample is a catalog-showroom store in which the customer selects items from a display or catalog to be delivered at a central checkout. All nine of the retailing organizations have stores throughout the Twin Cities metropolitan area, and for all but two of these firms, stores are located in both the city's center and the suburbs.

The Twin Cities are known internationally for their prominence in the field of designing and manufacturing electronic data-processing equipment. As one might suspect, this prominence has resulted in an industrial environment that includes not only the production of main-line computer and peripheral data-processing products but also the electronic components and parts used in manufacturing. Although not every one of the ten manufacturing organizations included here produce exclusively computer-related products, all but three manufacture items that are utilized in some aspect of the electronic data-processing industry. The three non-data-processing companies in our sample manufacture products such as electronically controlled appliances and medical equipment.

While nearly all sixteen of the hospitals in the sample can be considered general community hospitals, still considerable diversity exists among them. For instance, the sample includes both public (tax-supported) and private institutions and, among the private hospitals, both religiously affiliated and nonaffiliated hospitals. The participating hospitals are located in all parts of the metropolitan area: downtown, residential urban neighborhoods, and the suburbs. Although there is an underrepresentation of very small hospitals, there is still substantial variety with regard to the size of the institutions. The largest hospitals in the study employ nearly 3,500 individuals and contain 800 beds, while the smallest have approximately 700 employees and 200 beds.

It should be pointed out that all twenty-four labor unions and professional associations present in the thirty-five corporations included in the

Minneapolis-St. Paul study were contacted specifically and briefed on the project in the same way as the management of each corporation. Most of these unions and associations were supportive of the project although several did not wish to sponsor it officially. In no case, to our knowledge, was overt resistance exercised by the employee groups against the research, although in two cases (one a labor union and the other a professional employees' association) the group was firmly convinced of the potential worthlessness of our efforts.

Phase II

During Phase II, we broadened our study of employee theft and deviance to include two additional major metropolitan areas, Dallas-Fort Worth, Texas, and Cleveland, Ohio. An important consideration in selecting these two communities was the fact that their size, industries, and employee populations are approximately equal, in addition to representing two different geographical areas. However, the primary reason for specifically choosing these two communities was the wide differences in their officially reported rates of crime.

Our research design for Phase II called for us to test the hypothesis that the incidence of employee theft in a company is a direct reflection of the rate of nonviolent larceny in the larger community. The basic theoretical assumption is based upon the idea that if a company hires indigenous employees from that community, their aggregate theft behavior while at work may correspond to the level of theft present in the community. According to this design, one of the cities in the study should be a low- and the other a high-larceny city. Based upon information taken from the FBI's 1978 *Uniform Crime Reports,*[5] of the thirty-five largest metropolitan areas in the country, Cleveland ranked thirty-third with 2,127.8 larceny/thefts per 100,000 people. Dallas-Fort Worth ranked fifth highest in the country, reporting 4,106.1 incidents per 100,000 inhabitants. In addition, data collected from victimization studies in twenty-six of the same cities support the official statistics.[6] Cleveland ranked eighteenth with 85 thefts per 1,000 inhabitants.[7] The victimization studies indicated a rate of 116.5 (ranking ninth) for Dallas-Fort Worth—a rate almost half again as large as the incidence rate for Cleveland.[8] (Minneapolis-St. Paul ranked roughly midway between the two Phase II metropolitan areas on these indicators.)

Within each of these two communities, the Phase II research design concentrated on only two of the three industry sectors included in the Minneapolis-St. Paul study: retail stores and hospitals. The manufacturing sector was excluded from our plans for Phase II of the project because, in the formative stages of this research, we realized that finding two other communities with a similar level of specialization currently found in the Minneapolis-St. Paul electronics-manufacturing sector would be extremely difficult.

Further, budgetary constraints precluded our studying as many organizations in each Phase II community as we had in Minneapolis-St. Paul. Instead, we planned to survey approximately three of the largest organizations from each industry sector in both Dallas-Fort Worth and Cleveland. To gain entry into these organizations, we contacted by mail and telephone approximately five of the largest retailers and general hospitals in each community. We subsequently traveled to both communities and personally presented our research proposal to the executive officers of each targeted organization. The reader should note that, unlike Minnesota, the work forces in the vast majority of the organizations we contacted in Phase II are not unionized. The hospitals in Cleveland are an exception, in which case we also briefed the union on the design and goals of the project. Twelve firms eventually agreed to participate in the second phase of the research: seven retail stores (four in Dallas-Fort Worth, three in Cleveland) and five hospitals (two in Dallas-Fort Worth, three in Cleveland).

Since in Phase II we were mainly interested in involving large corporations, we focused on the major retail merchandise companies in each community. In Dallas-Fort Worth, three of the four participating retail organizations operate full-line department stores, while the fourth is more of a suburban self-service discount store. All four of these organizations have a number of stores located throughout the metropolitan area.

The retail sector in Cleveland includes two organizations that operate full-line department stores and one discount merchandiser. The two department-store corporations have stores both in downtown and suburban mall locations. The discounter, however, primarily has sites in suburban neighborhoods.

The hospital sector in Phase II is composed of five large general community hospitals—two in Dallas-Fort Worth and three in Cleveland. In Dallas-Fort Worth, one of the participating hospitals is a public, tax-supported institution, and the other is a religiously affiliated private hospital. Each of the Texas hospitals employs more than 2,000 individuals, and both are located in residential neighborhoods near the central business district.

Among the three hospitals studied in Cleveland, one is publicly supported and the other two are affiliates of religious denominations. The smallest of the three employs slightly over 1,500 individuals, while the largest has over 3,000 people on its payroll. All three of these hospitals are located in urban, residential neighborhoods.

The face-to-face employee-interview portion of the overall design was also implemented in Phase II, allowing the interviews to be guided by the preliminary findings of the Phase I (Minneapolis-St. Paul) survey. For purposes of data and analytical integration, organizations were selected from among corporations that already had been studied via questionnaire survey and organizational interviews in Phase I. Several criteria influenced our selection of specific firms for the qualitative study. For example, we concentrated on the larger organizations surveyed in Minneapolis-St. Paul in order to have a wide range of occupations represented in each firm's work force. The primary criterion, however, was the amount of theft found in each firm by the Phase I employee survey. In order to obtain the greatest insight into the processes leading to involvement in theft, we wanted to interview employees in each industry sector from an organization that had a high rate of self-reported theft and from a firm that had a low rate. Two organizations were selected from each of the three sectors—that is, two retail corporations, two hospitals, and two electronics-manufacturing firms. We approached these six corporations with the request that we be allowed to continue our research, and all six of the firms agreed.

Data-Collection Procedures

Three sources of data utilized in the study each required a separate and rather unique data-collection procedure. In the following section each of the three data-collection procedures is outlined.

Self-Report Questionnaire

In both phases of the research, after securing the active cooperation of the participating organizations, a random sample of employees at all levels of each firm was asked to respond to a mailed, self-administered questionnaire. The questionnaire asked employee respondents anonymously to provide data on personal and occupational characteristics, job satisfaction, perceptions of social controls deterring theft, and their personal involvement in a range of counterproductive and theft activities. The questionnaire booklet was designed to be self-administered in the privacy of one's home without the need of an interviewer.

Before selecting the self-report survey design, other direct data-collection techniques were considered but later rejected because of their particular limitations. Direct onsite observation, given the surreptitious nature and rarity of theft occurrences, would be extremely costly, both in terms of time and money, and would yield an unrepresentative sample. Having researchers pose as employees would also violate the employees' right to privacy and informed consent. Intensively interviewing employees from a single work group or company was incorporated (and is discussed later) as an important component of the total methodology, but the limitations in sample size, in addition to the anonymity-protection issues, prevented its use as the primary data-collection technique. The self-report survey technique was selected because it could afford the greatest anonymity protections to the participating employee and also yield the most reliable data, given the large numbers of employees and work settings that we desired to incorporate into the study.

We must point out that the self-report method has its own limitations. However, recent studies have shown that the obvious questions of response reliability and item validity are not as problematic as once believed. Regarding the question of reliability of the response when using this method, Hindelang and his associates report that a number of separate studies have demonstrated that test/retest or split-half checking procedures have consistently yielded quite respectable correlations on the order of .9.[9] Indeed, a study conducted by one of the authors has shown a relatively small amount of both under- and overreporting of deviance when reliability was verified via a polygraph examination.[10] While validity is significantly harder to establish, concurrent checks of official records,[11] studies using the known-group method,[12, 13] in addition to reports of informants,[14] have shown that self-reports also can yield substantially valid data.

The primary validity inadequacy of the self-report method concerns serious criminal behavior. When official data are compared to self-report results, the discrepancy noted between these two data sets is primarily attributable to the fact that the self-report instrument will underestimate the level of serious crime—particularly violent personal offenses.[15] This underestimation is perhaps why this technique has been used most extensively with various forms of nonserious deviant activity, most commonly adolescent delinquency. Accordingly, given the nonviolent nature of workplace deviance and lesser perceived seriousness of the harm associated with employee theft, we believe the self-report method can offer us far more, representative, and informative empirical data on the employee-deviance phenomenon than ever before achieved.

In order to draw a random sample of employees, we asked each organization to supply us with its most recent corporate mailing list. In most cases we obtained a complete mailing list, assigned each name a number, and randomly included employees in the sample by drawing four-digit numbers from a random number table. (A few organizations could only provide the project with a partially complete mailing list. In those instances, names were randomly excluded to generate the necessary sample.) For two hospitals, privacy regulations made it impossible to obtain access to a mailing list. In the first, the hospital provided a list of social security numbers. We drew a sample from those numbers and the hospital supplied us with the names and home addresses for those individuals. In the second, a government hospital would not release any home addresses but would provide names and work addresses. We sent letters describing the proposed research to one-third of that hospital's employees at work. A postcard was enclosed in each letter, and we asked the employees to write their home addresses on the cards and return them to us. Each person who returned a postcard was included in the survey. In all other cases a direct sampling of the mailing list was possible, although, as we shall see, some difficulties occurred from this procedure as well.

After a group of potential respondents had been selected for an organization, mailing labels and all survey materials were prepared by the research staff. Individuals in each organization received identical survey materials, and all materials were addressed "Dear (company name) employee." Respondents were told that their questionnaires could be identified as belonging to employees of a particular company but that actual names and addresses would remain confidential throughout the research process.

The mail-survey procedure in Phase I (Minneapolis-St. Paul) involved sending four pieces of mail:

1. An introductory letter explaining the project and its purpose. The letter also assured respondents of their anonymity and explained how their names were obtained.
2. The questionnaire and cover letter. The letter once again explained the project and assured anonymity. Also included with the questionnaire was a postage-paid return envelope.
3. A reminder postcard thanking those who had participated and asking those who had not returned the questionnaire to do so.
4. A replacement questionnaire and cover letter. The letter repeated our appreciation to those who had participated and asked them not to complete a second questionnaire. We reassured those who had not responded that the questionnaires were anonymous and asked them to consider participating.

Throughout the course of the survey, a local telephone number was available to all respondents through which a member of the research team could be reached to answer any questions a respondent might have. The reader should also note that we used slightly different questionnaire booklets and survey procedures in Phase II of the research. After Phase I was completed, we made internal and external reviews of the research process. As a result of these reviews, we slightly modified the survey instrument and design methodology in order to improve further the second phase of the project. In regard to the questionnaire instrument, we posed more-specific questions about personal involvement in theft activity. (The specific differences are discussed in more detail in the next chapter, which deals with the reported prevalence of employee theft.)

We also wanted to maximize the response rate in Phase II. Thus, we modified our design methodoly to be consistent with Dillman's Total Design Method of mailed survey research.[16] While in Phase I we sent the questionnaires and the follow-up reminders by nonprofit-permit bulk mail, in Phase II, using Dillman's recommended techniques, the initial and follow-up mailings went first class. We also added mail-control numbers to the questionnaire booklets that allowed us to direct the follow-ups only to those who had not responded. The survey process still involved sending four pieces of mail. However, the introductory letter was eliminated and a second replacement questionnaire was added. This final reminder was sent by certified mail to ensure that our mailings reached every person who was sampled.

During the two phases of this research project, 9,175 employees returned questionnaires, or 53.8 percent of those sampled. In the first phase of the study, a total of 4,985 individuals (or 50.8 percent of those sampled) returned completed questionnaires, and of those who were sampled in Phase II, 4,190 (or 57.9 percent) returned completed booklets. Based upon accepted standards of survey research, this return rate was not as high as originally we had hoped. Social scientists usually feel the most confidence in their survey results when they have reached at least the 70 percent return-rate level.[17] Our return rate undoubtedly was diminished by a long questionnaire booklet, a sensitive topic, and most important, unforeseen inaccuracies in the mailing lists provided to us by the participating organizations. Specifically, the rate of return was depressed artificially by high turnover among the work forces in the surveyed organizations, particularly in the retail and hospital industries. As a result, some of the people we sampled terminated their jobs over the course of the survey procedure and may well have had little interest (or felt it inappropriate) to complete a questionnaire about their past employer.

Because this type of sample attrition is not usually a problem in surveys of the general population that have received response rates of 70 percent or higher, we felt it necessary to estimate its net effect on our final return rate. While we do not have data on the extent of attrition among the samples from Phase I organizations, we do have data for Phase II. At the end of the survey procedure in Phase II, we systematically compared our mailing lists with current payroll records in five randomly selected organizations to see how many nonrespondents had terminated employment since the mailing list was created. In those five firms, when the terminees were removed from the sample, the adjusted return rate was at least 74 percent in the first organization, 69 percent in the second organization, 66 percent in the third organization, 75 percent in the fourth organization, and 56 percent in the fifth organization.

From this examination of mailing-list accuracy, when former employees are removed from the sample using the turnover criteria supplied by the organizations, we estimate the adjusted return rate to be as high as 65-75 percent. We mention this because we do not believe that the accuracy of the conclusions drawn from these data is significantly affected by the artificially depressed actual rate of return. On the contrary, given the unaccounted for high attrition in the sample, we have the same degree of confidence in our data as if we had reached the adjusted rates of return similar to a survey of the general population.

Executive Interviews

Within the forty-seven participating organizations, we conducted personal interviews with key management executives. In particular, we wanted to learn about each organization's emphasis on the dissemination of antitheft policies, the control of materials and money, screening of prospective employees, and the deterrent effect of security operations. In Phase I we completed 180 interviews with executives of the thirty-five participating firms, and 67 interviews were conducted in the twelve organizations studied in Phase II, yielding a total of 247 corporate managers.

The reader should note that in Minneapolis-St. Paul we went to each of the participating organizations in person to conduct the interviews. Due to budgetary constraints, the interviews with organization executives in Dallas-Fort Worth and Cleveland were conducted by long-distance telephone after considerable initial contact and scheduling of the interview. As a result, for Phase II, we refined the interview guides and made the questions more concise so that the telephone time required for the interview would be minimized. In both phases, however, the interviews solicited essentially the same information.

Although we completed 247 interviews during the two phases of this research, we must point out that the executive interviews rely heavily on verbal evaluations and off-the-cuff personal assessments by members of the management team. However, given the variety in the corporate-management responses to the problem of employee theft, we feel confident in our ability to differentiate among participating organizations, both among and within industry sectors.

Face-to-Face Employee Interviews

In order to conduct direct interviews with an organization's work force, a personal letter was sent to a mailing list of about 100 randomly selected employees (excluding any employee formerly sampled in the study) from each of the six corporations. The letters informed the employee of the nature of the research and the confidentiality and anonymity of their voluntary participation. Enclosed in each letter was a stamped, self-addressed postcard that, if they agreed to be interviewed, employees were asked to sign, list their telephone number and occupational category, and return to the university project office. Over one-third of the sampled employees did so, and they became a pool from which the initial interviewees were drawn. This voluntary sample was supplemented via a purposive snowball method in the interest of achieving broader coverage with unrepresented occupational categories and physical locations within each work place. Together, the two sources of respondents served to provide an adequate number and variety of employee persectives and experiences. During the qualitative portion of the research, we conducted 256 personal interviews: 87 in the retail sector, 79 in the hospital sector, and 90 in the manufacturing sector.

Three researchers were involved in the employee-interview process, each focusing his efforts on a single industry sector. The overall thrust represented an unusual team approach to qualitative research, in contrast to the more-typical so-called Lone Ranger approach wherein a single researcher pursues a phenomenon of interest. Although the Lone Ranger approach has produced many enlightening and important works, some scholars and practitioners point to its limitations. Specifically, the solitary researcher who seeks an in-depth examination of a complex social phenomenon must necessarily restrict the scope of her or his study, thereby possibly limiting its full theoretical contribution and its generalizability. The team approach, however, provides a framework in which the quality of data received can be improved through extensive debate, cross-checking, stimulation, and support. Frequent interaction among team members regarding issues of field operations, interview techniques, interview substance, and so forth was strongly encouraged throughout the data-collection and -analysis phases.

Relevant literature reviews and preliminary results obtained from exploratory qualitative studies between the first and second phases provided us with the specific scholarly and policy areas of interest for the interviews. Our basic objectives for the employee-interview portion of the study were:

> To understand the patterns of individual, occupational, and organizational behavior (that is, the processes that explain the quality and quantity of worker deviance);

> To understand more thoroughly the specific correlates of employee property and production deviance;

> To capture the meanings of worker deviance in the work setting;

To assure the validity of findings derived through other data sources and methods in the study.

Although the employee interviews were focused specifically, they certainly remained open ended or unconstricted enough to permit freedom for interviewees to introduce topics of their choosing into the conversation. The phenomenon of primary interest, employee theft, was broached through a procedure often referred to as card sorting. Midway through each interview, respondents were given a set of approximately thirty cards containing brief descriptions of possible deviant activities commonly associated with their particular work environment. (The specific items included in the card sort are presented in table 3-11.) The cards depicted two types of deviance—namely, the misuse of production time and the misuse of property. Each respondent was asked to sort the cards according to whether or not he or she was aware of their occurrence. Interviewees were cautioned to identify as occurring only those activities they personally knew had happened in their place of current employment. Following the card sort, respondents were asked several sets of questions designed to illuminate the nature and process of the activities identified as occurring.

These face-to-face employee interviews, like our other two sources of data, are not without their limitations. Since we interviewed a small number of individuals, it was not possible for us to talk with employees from every area of an organization. Moreover, our initial method of contacting employees by mail allowed them to self-select themselves into the sample. Thus, we recognize that opinions expressed during these interviews may not be truly representative of the perceptions of each industry's work force. However, by using the snowball sample to help to insure adequate coverage of each organization and by studying two separate organizations in each sector, the interviews provided us with unique insight into the processes by which people become involved in theft and other types of work-place deviant behavior.

Conclusion

This research methodology allowed us to collect an impressive amount of data on employee theft and deviance over a three-year period. The remaining chapters are an attempt to provide an overview of this information. We have liberally interlaced data and findings collected from our three sources—self-report employee questionnaires, executive interviews, and face-to-face employee interviews. With this information we now address the hypotheses introduced in chapter 1.

Notes

1. D. Merriam, "Employee Theft," *Criminal Justice Abstracts* 9 (1977):380-386.

2. G. Robin, "Employees as Offenders," *Journal of Research on Crime and Delinquency* 6 (1969):17-33.

3. Alice P. Franklin, *Internal Theft in a Retail Organization: A Case Study* (Ann Arbor, Mich.: University Microfilms, 1975).

4. Richard C. Hollinger, *Employee Deviance: Acts against the Formal Work Organization* (Ann Arbor, Mich.: University Microfilms, 1979).

5. Federal Bureau of Investigation, William H. Webster, director, *Crime in the United States—1978* (Washington, D.C.: U.S. Department of Justice, 1979).

6. U.S. Department of Justice, Law Enforcement Assistance Administration, *Criminal Victimization Surveys in Eight American Cities* (Washington D.C.: Government Printing Office, 1976).

7. Ibid.

8. Ibid.

9. M.J. Hindelang, T. Hirschi, and Joseph G. Weis, "Correlates of Delinquency: The Illusion of Discrepancy between Self-Report and Official Measures," *American Sociological Review* 44 (1979):995-1014.

10. J.P. Clark and L.L. Tifft, "Polygraph and Interview Validation of Self-Reported Deviant Behavior," *American Sociological Review* 31 (1966):516-523.

11. R. Hardt and S. Peterson-Hardt, "On Determining the Quality of the Delinquency Self-Report Method," *Journal of Research in Crime and Delinquency* 14 (1977):247-261.

12. Ivan Nye, *Family Relationships and Delinquent Behavior* (New York: Wiley and Sons, 1958).

13. M. Erickson and L.T. Empey, "Court Records, Undetected Delinquency, and Decision Making," *Journal of Criminal Law, Criminology and Police Science* 54 (1963):456-469.

14. Martin Gold, *Delinquent Behavior in an American City* (Belmont, Calif.: Brooks/Cole, 1970).

15. Hindelang, Hirschi, and Weiss, "Correlates of Delinquency."

16. Don A. Dillman, *Mail and Telephone Surveys: The Total Design Method* (New York: Wiley and Sons, 1978).

17. W. Goudy, "Interim Response to a Mail Questionnaire: Impacts on Variable Relationships," *The Sociological Quarterly* 19 (1978):253-265.

3

Prevalence of Employee Deviance

The fundamental question this book first attempted to answer was: How much employee deviance, particularly property theft, occurs in a typical retail store, hospital, or manufacturing plant? As we discussed in chapter 1, very little comprehensive data is currently available about deviant work-place activities. This paucity of information exists for a very good reason—employee deviance, by definition, is normally hidden from the view of fellow workers, the general public, and also social-science researchers. Further, it is not a simple matter to impose a standard definition of theft or deviance upon the great variety of circumstances in which employees appear to violate behavioral rules. In order to remedy this situation, we designed our research effort to assemble what information is presently available and to develop new and innovative data-collection strategies. In this chapter, we present what we have learned about employee deviance, utilizing three sources of data: (1) estimates by organizational executives, (2) self-report questionnaire survey results, and (3) face-to-face employee interviews.

Organizational Estimates of Property Deviance

As noted in chapter 2, our preliminary research told us that organizations have little exact knowledge regarding the extent of employee theft. This finding was confirmed by our interviews with corporate executives. During these interviews, we sought to obtain information that would indicate how much theft was occurring in each of the forty-seven participating organizations. Although organizational officials could not be expected to know which specific individuals were perpetrating theft, we thought that they might have some measure of the aggregate effects of employees' stealing. In particular, we asked for two sources of corporate data from each firm that could indicate the pervasiveness of theft: (1) security records and (2) inventory-shrinkage rates.

Security Records

Reports of theft incidents were the first type of security-department record we examined. Typically, when either organizational property or an employee's personal property is unaccounted for and theft is suspected, an incident report is filed with the security office. From these records we hoped to determine how much theft within an organization during the last calendar year was attributable to employees. Unfortunately, the use of these reports was unproductive in all three industry sectors. At best, the security departments in the hospitals, manufacturing firms, and retail stores in our study could only give us the total number of thefts of all types discovered within a company. Since the actual perpertrator of the vast majority of these incidents was never identified, there was no way of knowing what portion of the total number of reported thefts was committed by employees when compared to those committed by nonemployees.

Since examining the number of formally reported occurrences of employee theft was not possible, we turned to an alternate corporate-security statistic—namely, the annual number of theft apprehensions. Again, problems arose with this measurement of the prevalence of theft. First, nearly half of the organizations had not maintained thorough enough records to reveal how many employees had been apprehended. More often than not, we found no centralized summary of employees who had been caught stealing. The only place where information might exist about an employee's participation in theft was on a termination notice that was kept in the individual's personnel file. Because reasons for termination often were kept vague due to the legal defamation-of-character implications, this was also not a useful data source on employee-theft prevalence.

Another complication associated with using apprehension records to measure the amount of theft was discovered—namely, these records may be more a function of the departments' reaction than the employees' offending. In other words, employee-theft apprehension rates, like arrest rates generally, often are more a reflection of policing practices than the actual criminal behavior. Thus, to use apprehension records as an indicator of employee-theft prevalence in organizations would lead to serious problems of validity and reliability. These data are important, however, since in chapter 8 we utilize them as an independent variable to determine whether apprehending employees is a deterrent to theft.

Inventory Shrinkage

As noted in chapter 1, a company's inventory-shrinkage rate represents the inventory deficit in dollars that cannot be accounted for after reductions for sales and unsold stock have been subtracted. Many factors other than internal theft (for example, shoplifting, bookkeeping error, spoilage, and breakage) can affect the magnitude of inventory shrinkage. Nonetheless, the figure does partially reflect losses due to theft, but the question is which part.

Several serious problems were associated with our using inventory-shrinkage statistics as a measure of the extent of employee theft. First, not all the firms included in the study (such as manufacturers and hospitals) calculated such a figure. Second, some organizations produced shortage statistics only for certain departments. For example, hospitals commonly calculate a shortage only for the main storeroom, central supply, and pharmacy. Third, not all firms used the same formula in deriving the figures. Even in retail the data were not totally comparable.

Thus, as we had suspected, official organizational sources of data on theft involvement were not uniformly available within each of our forty-seven organizations. (This issue is discussed more thoroughly in chapter 8.) Instead, we were forced to focus heavily on the self-reported involvement of employees to measure the prevalence of both property and production deviance.

Self-Reported Deviance of Employees

A self-administered questionnaire survey of employees in the retail, hospital, and electronics-manufacturing industries provided us with acceptable data to test the various hypotheses about the phenomenon of employee theft and other forms of work-place deviance. Via a questionnaire booklet, each respondent was presented with a list of specific examples of work-place deviant behavior. We requested that the respondents anonymously indicate by circling choices on the questionnaire the extent of their involvement in each activity.

The items of deviant behavior corresponding to property deviance dealt with specific acts of theft of property belonging to the company, fellow workers, or outsiders (for example, customers in retail stores or patients in hospitals). Some of the property-deviance items of necessity varied by industry sector because of the substantial differences in the nature of property among the three industries—that is, articles that can be taken by employees in a retail store differ rather dramatically from those things a hospital or electronics-manufacturing worker can take. Thus, in the retail-sector questionnaire we included items about misusing the discount privilege, taking or damaging merchandise (to buy it later at a discount), and underringing purchases, while in the hospital sector we asked about the taking of supplies, medication, and equipment. Manufacturing employees were surveyed about the theft of precious metals, raw materials, and finished products. Obviously, one of the consequences of this necessary procedure is to make direct comparisons of employee theft across industry sectors impossible.

The examples of deviant behavior also included counterproductive behavior, which refers to acts by employees that violate corporate policy regulating the use of time and the amount or quality of work accomplished. Incorporated under this heading are activities such as doing slow or sloppy work and coming to work under the influence of alcohol or drugs. Since it was felt that participating in these behaviors was possible for all employees regardless of occupation or industry, the same five items were included on each sector's questionnaire. (A third category of behavior, positive deviance, was also included in the Minneapolis-St. Paul questionnaire. This category refers to those items that measure activities that exceed formal requirements for the job—for example, doing work above and beyond the call of duty.)

The specific items developed to measure various forms of employee deviance in the retail and hospital sectors in Minneapolis-St. Paul, Dallas-Fort Worth, and Cleveland, and in the manufacturing sector in Minneapolis-St. Paul, are listed in tables 3-1 through 3-7. These tables also indicate the reported levels of respondent participation by item.

The reader should note from these tables that slightly more deviant involvement was reported by the Minneapolis-St. Paul Phase I sample than by the Dallas-Fort Worth and Cleveland Phase II samples. Although many factors may have contributed to this difference, we believe it was primarily the result of asking Phase II respondents about their activity within a specific rather than a general time period. When we surveyed employees in Minneapolis and St. Paul, we asked them to indicate how often they engaged in each of the items of deviant behavior. The possible response choices were almost daily, weekly, monthly, yearly, happened once, not applicable, and never. As was noted earlier, for the Dallas-Fort Worth and Cleveland phase of the study, we modified the survey instrument to obtain more information about the frequency of employee involvement in theft and other counterproductive activities. To this end, we asked respondents how many times they had committed each act within the past year and gave the following response choices: almost daily, about once a week, about once a month, between four and eleven times, two or three times, once, and never.

The reader should also note that in Dallas-Fort Worth and Cleveland we asked more-detailed questions about the theft of company property. This was done to ensure that property deviance was measured better across the entire range of employees. For example, in Minneapolis-St. Paul, one of the items on the hospital questionnaire dealt with the taking of hospital supplies, and retail employees were asked one question about merchandise theft. For the Dallas-Fort Worth and Cleveland study, we asked hospital respondents several questions about particular kinds of supplies—for example, clerical, janitorial, linen, and patient care. We also divided the retail-merchandise item into two questions: merchandise worth less than $5 and merchandise worth more than $5. Thus, the reader is cautioned not to com-

Table 3-1
Percentage of Minneapolis-St. Paul Retail Employees Responding to Deviance Items

How Often Do You Engage in Each Activity?	Daily	Weekly	Monthly	Yearly	Happened Once	Never	Not Applicable	Total Valid Cases
Take unauthorized long lunch or coffee breaks	12.5	21.6	18.7	5.2	9.4	26.9	5.7	1,372
Give up lunch or coffee breaks in order to work	16.9	28.1	19.9	5.3	8.9	18.7	2.2	1,372
Punch a time card for an absent employee	0.2	0.2	0.5	0.3	1.9	86.3	10.6	1,375
Do slow or sloppy work on purpose	0.4	2.3	6.5	4.9	5.4	78.1	2.4	1,375
Work under the influence of alcohol or drugs	0.6	1	2.3	2.1	4.4	88.6	1	1,374
Use the discount privileges to buy merchandise for nonemployees	1.2	5.5	21.7	16	12.8	41.6	1.2	1,375
Take unauthorized money or gifts from business clients	0.1	0.2	0.7	1.6	2.6	74.3	20.5	1,375
Come to work late or leave early without approval	0.8	4.6	13.2	7.5	10.7	60.2	3	1,375
Take store merchandise	0.3	0.8	2.3	2.5	5.9	85.7	2.5	1,374
Use sick leave when not sick	—	0.1	3.9	8.2	9.7	62.3	15.8	1,375
Get paid for more hours than were worked	0.1	0.5	1.5	2.3	4.7	85	5.9	1,374
Damage merchandise so that you can buy it on discount	—	0.1	0.4	0.7	1.1	90.2	7.5	1,377
Work extra hours without overtime pay or other rewards	5	11	14.1	7.6	7.3	48.7	6.3	1,373
Are reimbursed for more money than spent on business expenses	0.4	0.2	0.9	1.5	1.2	48.4	47.4	1,372
Purposely underring purchases	0.2	0.4	2.1	1	1.9	68.5	25.9	1,373
Borrow or take money from employer without authorization	0.1	0.1	0.4	0.4	1.1	85.2	12.7	1,375
Take personal property of co-workers or nonemployees	—	0.1	0.1	0.1	0.5	97.5	1.7	1,377
Shortchange or overcharge customers	0.4	0.9	2.1	3.2	7.8	63.1	22.5	1,370
Fail to report theft of employer's property	0.4	0.6	1.6	2.1	4	83.5	7.8	1,366
Do work above and beyond the call of duty	21.4	28	24.6	7.6	3.7	11.8	2.9	1,368

Table 3-2
Percentage of Dallas-Fort Worth Retail Employees Responding to Deviance Items

Within the Past Year, How Many Times Did You	Almost Daily	About Once a Week	About Once a Month	Between Four and Eleven Times	Two or Three Times	Once	Never	Total Valid Cases
Take a long lunch or coffee break without approval?	3	7.3	7	5.8	19.6	8.8	48.5	1,303
Fill out or punch a time card for an absent employee?	0.1	0.4	0.3	—	1.2	1.1	96.9	1,308
Do slow or sloppy work on purpose?	0.2	0.9	1.1	1.4	6.9	5.3	84.2	1,309
Come to work while under the influence of alcohol or drugs?	0.4	0.6	0.4	0.7	2.1	3.4	92.4	1,310
Use the discount privilege in an unauthorized manner?	0.4	0.3	0.9	2	5.1	5.4	85.9	1,310
Take office or clerical supplies?	0.2	0.4	0.2	0.8	4.7	5	88.7	1,307
Take an item of store merchandise with a retail value of $5 or less?	—	0.1	0.1	0.2	1.3	2.3	96	1,309
Take an item of store merchandise with a retail value of more than $5?	—	0.2	0.1	—	0.7	0.8	98.2	1,309
Take unauthorized money or gifts from a vendor or supplier?	0.1	0.1	0.1	0.2	0.8	1.5	97.2	1,308
Come to work late or leave early without approval?	0.7	3	3.3	5.4	13.3	8.3	66	1,306
Purposely underring a customer's purchase?	0.1	0.2	—	0.2	0.9	0.8	97.8	1,297
Use sick leave when not sick?	0.1	0.1	0.5	2.2	6.1	8.2	82.8	1,306
Get paid for more hours than were worked?	0.2	0.2	0.2	0.3	1.3	2.4	95.4	1,310
Damage an item of merchandise in order to buy it on discount?	—	—	—	0.2	0.2	0.5	99.1	1,308
Be reimbursed for more money than spent on business expenses?	—	0.2	0.1	0.1	0.3	0.5	98.8	1,303
Take company equipment or tools?	—	0.1	—	0.1	0.8	1.1	97.9	1,309
Borrow or take money from employer?	—	—	0.2	0.5	1.6	1.3	96.4	1,305
Take personal property of co-workers or customers?	—	0.1	—	—	0.1	0.1	99.7	1,311
Shortchange or overcharge a customer on purpose?	—	0.1	0.1	0.1	0.3	0.4	99	1,304
Ignore an instance of pilferage or shoplifting?	0.1	0.1	0.1	0.2	1.2	2.4	95.9	1,306

Table 3-3
Percentage of Cleveland Retail Employees Responding to Deviance Items

Within the Past Year, How Many Times Did You	Almost Daily	About Once a Week	About Once a Month	Between Four and Eleven Times	Two or Three Times	Once	Never	Total Valid Cases
Take a long lunch or coffee break without approval?	3.7	8.8	7.9	6.7	17	8.6	47.3	822
Fill out or punch a time card for an absent employee?	0.2	0.4	0.1	0.5	0.8	1.1	96.9	826
Do slow or sloppy work on purpose?	0.2	0.8	1.5	1.2	6.3	3.8	86.2	827
Come to work while under the influence of alcohol or drugs?	0.6	0.8	0.5	1	1.6	3.1	92.4	828
Use the discount privilege in an unauthorized manner?	0.1	0.7	1.8	4.2	7.4	4.3	81.5	827
Take office or clerical supplies?	—	0.8	0.6	1.1	5.2	3.9	88.4	828
Take an item of store merchandise with a retail value of $5 or less?	0.4	0.2	0.2	0.4	2.4	3	93.4	828
Take an item of store merchandise with a retail value of more than $5?	—	0.6	0.2	—	0.4	0.7	98.1	826
Take unauthorized money or gifts from a vendor or supplier?	—	—	0.7	0.2	1.6	1.5	96	825
Come to work late or leave early without approval?	1.5	2.1	4.6	5.3	11.9	5.6	69	825
Purposely underring a customer's purchase?	0.1	0.1	0.5	0.5	0.9	0.5	97.4	819
Use sick leave when not sick?	0.2	0.1	1.6	2.4	7.1	7.7	80.9	823
Get paid for more hours than were worked?	0.4	0.5	0.7	1.1	1.8	3.4	92.1	826
Damage an item of merchandise in order to buy it on discount?	0.1	0.1	—	0.1	0.6	0.5	98.6	827
Be reimbursed for more money than spent on business expenses?	—	—	0.4	—	0.6	0.5	98.5	816
Take company equipment or tools?	0.1	—	—	0.6	0.5	2.3	96.5	826
Borrow or take money from employer?	0.1	0.4	0.1	0.2	0.9	1.7	96.6	825
Take personal property of co-workers or customers?	—	—	0.1	0.2	—	0.2	99.5	827
Shortchange or overcharge a customer on purpose?	—	0.2	0.1	0.2	0.4	0.5	98.6	821
Ignore an instance of pilferage or shoplifting?	0.2	—	0.2	0.7	1.7	3.1	94.1	821

Table 3-4
Percentage of Minneapolis-St. Paul Hospital Employees Responding to Deviance Items

How Often Do You Engage in Each Activity?	Daily	Weekly	Monthly	Yearly	Happened Once	Never	Not Applicable	Total Valid Cases
Take unauthorized long lunch or coffee breaks	14.1	19.6	21.7	7.1	4.6	25.3	7.6	2,025
Give up lunch or coffee breaks in order to work	19.8	34	25.1	4.4	4.4	9.6	2.7	2,031
Punch a time card for an absent employee	0.4	0.5	0.6	0.6	1.8	60.5	35.6	2,040
Do slow or sloppy work on purpose	0.3	1.2	5.5	3.5	4.4	82.9	2.2	2,040
Work under the influence of alcohol or drugs	0.2	0.4	0.7	1.2	3.4	92.5	1.6	2,043
Take hospital supplies (for example, bandages, thermometers, linens)	0.2	1	9.4	13.3	13	60	3.1	2,034
Take unauthorized money or gifts from business clients	0.1	0.1	0.3	1.6	2.5	76.4	19	2,042
Come to work late or leave early without approval	1.2	4.6	11.2	10.2	8.4	61.3	3.1	2,039
Take or use medication intended for patients	0.1	0.5	2	3.7	3.5	77.6	12.6	2,037
Use sick leave when not sick	—	0.3	6.5	24.6	16.4	49.8	2.4	2,034
Get paid for more hours than were worked	0.3	0.6	2.2	2.4	4	87	3.5	2,041
Take or eat hospital food without paying for it	5.9	9.7	10.9	4.9	3.9	58.4	6.3	2,035
Work extra hours without overtime pay or other rewards	8.4	17.8	20.7	8.7	4.3	37.5	2.6	2,038
Are reimbursed for more money than spent on business expenses	0.1	0.1	0.3	0.5	0.9	48.9	49.2	2,038
Take hospital tools or equipment	—	0.1	0.5	3.3	4.1	87.2	4.8	2,041
Borrow or take money from employer without authorization	—	—	0.1	0.1	0.4	80.2	19.2	2,042
Take personal property of co-workers or nonemployees	—	—	0.1	0.3	0.6	97.9	1.1	2,309
Charge one patient for services or medication given to another	0.2	1.8	2.5	2.7	2.4	63.8	26.6	2,037
Fail to report theft of employer's property	1.2	0.8	2.7	2.9	2.5	78.4	11.5	2,017
Do work above and beyond the call of duty	19.9	25.6	27.8	9.8	3.2	9.7	4	2,011

Table 3-5
Percentage of Dallas-Fort Worth Hospital Employees Responding to Deviance Items

Within the Past Year, How Many Times Did You	Almost Daily	About Once a Week	About Once a Month	Between Four and Eleven Times	Two or Three Times	Once	Never	Total Valid Cases
Take a long lunch or coffee break without approval?	2.9	9.1	6.6	4.9	19.7	7.3	49.5	899
Fill out or punch a time card for an absent employee?	0.2	0.2	0.2	0.2	0.4	0.8	98	907
Do slow or sloppy work on purpose?	0.1	0.5	1.3	1.7	4.5	2.3	89.6	906
Come to work while under the influence of alcohol or drugs?	0.1	0.6	0.7	0.3	1.1	1.3	95.9	907
Take patient-care supplies?	0.1	0.1	0.7	0.9	4.7	3.4	90.1	907
Take office or clerical supplies?	0.4	0.6	1	1.7	7.3	5.6	83.4	904
Take housekeeping or janitorial supplies?	—	0.2	0.5	0.1	2.3	1.4	95.5	908
Take linens, uniforms, or gowns?	—	—	0.2	0.4	3.2	5.6	90.6	905
Take unauthorized money or gifts from a vendor or supplier?	—	—	0.5	0.1	0.3	1	98.1	904
Come to work late or leave early without approval?	0.6	3	3.3	3.8	10	7	72.3	900
Take or use medication intended for patients?	—	0.3	0.7	1.2	3.6	3	91.2	905
Use sick leave when not sick?	—	0.2	1.1	2.7	12.1	10.6	73.3	904
Get paid for more hours than were worked?	—	0.6	0.2	0.2	2.4	2	94.6	905
Take or eat food intended for patients?	1.3	1	2	3.4	5.6	4.7	82	904
Be reimbursed for more money than spent on business expenses?	—	—	—	—	—	0.7	99.2	902
Take hospital equipment or tools?	—	0.1	—	0.2	1.6	2.2	95.7	905
Borrow or take money from employer?	—	0.3	—	0.1	1.9	1.8	95.5	908
Take personal property of co-workers or patients?	0.1	0.1	—	—	0.1	0.1	99.6	908
Take hospital property with a value of $5 or more?	—	0.2	—	0.2	1.1	1.1	97.4	908
Ignore an instance of pilferage?	1.5	0.7	1.2	1.1	4.3	2.5	88.7	886

Table 3-6
Percentage of Cleveland Hospital Employees Responding to Deviance Items

Within the Past Year, How Many Times Did You	Almost Daily	About Once a Week	About Once a Month	Between Four and Eleven Times	Two or Three Times	Once	Never	Total Valid Cases
Take a long lunch or coffee break without approval?	2.5	5.7	8.2	6	19.6	8.2	49.8	1,077
Fill out or punch a time card for an absent employee?	0.2	0.2	0.3	0.2	0.9	0.9	97.3	1,085
Do slow or sloppy work on purpose?	0.1	0.4	1.2	1.1	5.4	2.3	89.5	1,091
Come to work while under the influence of alcohol or drugs?	0.1	0.2	0.1	0.1	0.9	1.3	97.3	1,090
Take patient-care supplies?	0.1	0.2	0.8	0.6	6.3	3.5	88.5	1,085
Take office or clerical supplies?	0.1	0.4	1	1.8	9.8	6.5	80.4	1,088
Take housekeeping or janitorial supplies?	—	—	0.4	0.3	1.1	1.4	96.8	1,086
Take linens, uniforms, or gowns?	—	0.3	0.2	0.3	2.9	5.3	91	1,087
Take unauthorized money or gifts from a vendor or supplier?	—	0.1	—	0.1	0.5	1.3	98	1,087
Come to work late or leave early without approval?	0.9	1.7	3.9	4.8	12.1	6.1	70.5	1,085
Take or use medication intended for patients?	0.1	0.1	0.5	1.4	3.4	3.3	91.2	1,081
Use sick leave when not sick?	—	—	1.5	4.1	17	12.2	65.2	1,087
Get paid for more hours than were worked?	0.2	0.2	0.6	0.8	2	1.9	94.3	1,088
Take or eat food intended for patients?	0.7	0.9	1.1	1.4	4.6	2.3	89	1,084
Be reimbursed for more money than spent on business expenses?	—	—	—	0.2	0.2	0.5	99.1	1,078
Take hospital equipment or tools?	0.2	—	0.1	0.3	2.1	1.9	95.4	1,083
Borrow or take money from employer?	—	0.1	—	0.1	0.9	1.6	97.3	1,085
Take personal property of co-workers or patients?	—	—	—	—	—	0.2	99.8	1,086
Take hospital property with a value of $5 or more?	0.1	0.2	—	0.2	1.4	0.9	97.2	1,087
Ignore an instance of pilferage?	1.2	0.4	0.9	1.6	5	4	86.9	1,067

Table 3-7
Percentage of Minneapolis-St. Paul Manufacturing Employees Responding to Deviance Items

How Often Do You Engage in Each Activity?	Daily	Weekly	Monthly	Yearly	Happened Once	Never	Not Applicable	Total Valid Cases
Take unauthorized long lunch or coffee breaks	18	23.5	22	7.2	4.6	19.9	4.8	1,470
Give up lunch or coffee breaks in order to work	19.7	27.3	19	3.9	6.3	21.6	2.2	1,474
Take metals used in production (for example, platinum, gold, copper)	0.1	0.1	0.5	1	1.4	67.7	29.2	1,472
Do slow or sloppy work on purpose	0.5	1.3	5.7	4.4	4.3	81.5	2.3	1,467
Work under the influence of alcohol or drugs	1.1	1.3	3.1	6.4	6.4	80.1	1.6	1,474
Take other materials used in production (raw materials, components)	0.1	0.4	3.5	9.7	7.3	66.2	12.8	1,470
Take unauthorized money or gifts from business clients	—	0.1	0.4	1.8	1.1	73.6	23	1,471
Come to work late or leave early without approval	1.9	9	19.4	12.2	7.6	45.3	4.6	1,471
Discuss confidential company information with nonemployees	0.9	0.9	2.5	5.6	3	72.9	14.2	1,467
Use sick leave when not sick	—	0.2	9.6	26.6	10.9	45.8	6.9	1,473
Get paid for more hours than were worked	0.2	0.5	2.9	4.8	3.7	79.4	8.5	1,473
Use unauthorized computer time for personal reasons	0.3	1	2.2	3	1.6	63.2	28.7	1,470
Work extra hours without overtime pay or other rewards	10	16.6	18.5	6.9	4.2	40.1	3.7	1,471
Are reimbursed for more money than spent on business expenses	0.1	0.6	1.4	5.5	2.4	57	33	1,471
Take company tools or equipment	—	0.1	1.1	6.9	8.6	77.5	5.8	1,472
Borrow or take money from employer without authorization	—	—	0.2	0.4	0.3	81.9	17.2	1,473
Take personal property of co-workers or nonemployees	—	—	0.1	0.1	0.2	98.2	1.4	1,471
Take products manufactured by the company	—	—	0.4	2.2	3.9	89	4.5	1,471
Fail to report theft of employer's property	1.8	1.1	2.4	3.7	3.9	75.4	11.7	1,453
Do work above and beyond the call of duty	16.2	25.2	27.1	12	3.4	13	3.1	1,455

pare directly the percentage of people involved in a specific activity in Minneapolis-St. Paul with the percentage involved in Dallas-Forth Worth and Cleveland. Due to instrument similarities within Phase II, the responses from Dallas-Fort Worth and Cleveland can be compared directly, however.

Property-Deviance Dependent Variable

Because of the differing nature of the deviant behaviors included on the questionnaire, not all of the items could be used as an employee-theft dependent variable for this study. Conversely, no single item encompassed enough of the possible manifestations of theft behavior to stand alone as the dependent variable. Thus, it was necessary to construct three specific indexes to represent the phenomenon of employee theft for each industry. Before we could create each sector's index, however, we had to make adjustments due to item and response-choice differences between Phase I and Phase II.

First, responses from Phase I had to be adapted to reflect involvement within one year's time so as to conform with the time frame used in Phase II. This was done by recoding the responses of the Minneapolis-St. Paul employees who answered "happened once." If a respondent indicated that he or she had been involved in an activity once and had worked for the participating organization less than one year, then the response was recorded as "yearly." If the respondent had worked for the firm more than one year, the response was recorded as "never." This left us five response categories: (1) daily, (2) weekly, (3) monthly, (4) yearly, and (5) never/not applicable. ("Never" and "not applicable" were combined because both responses indicate that the employee was not involved in an activity.) In Phase II, however, we used seven response categories. Thus, the responses from Dallas-Fort Worth and Cleveland were collapsed into five classifications into which the Minneapolis-St. Paul responses also could be incorporated: (1) almost daily, (2) about once a week, (3) between four and twelve times a year, (4) one to three times a year, and (5) never. In addition, for the Dallas-Fort Worth and Cleveland respondents, we consolidated the four supply items in the hospital sector and the two merchandise items in retail stores into single supply and merchandise items. This was necessary since only one question was asked about each subject in Phase I.

By making these adjustments in the data, we could combine the responses from both phases of the research. The question then became which of the items should be included in the index measuring employee theft. Due to the nature of the deviant behaviors, relatively small amounts of admitted behavior were reported for each of the items, making traditional methods of scale or index development using statistical criteria impossible. Instead, judgments concerning the inclusion of an item in the index were based upon face validity using the following criteria:

Selection included only those items that were thefts of goods, materials, or money.

Items could be included only if they were asked in both phases of the research (for example, taking clerical supplies in retail was only asked in Phase II).

Items that were not thefts victimizing one's employer were excluded (for example, taking personal property of co-workers or nonemployees).

Items were excluded that, due to varying organizational policies, were questionable as to whether they were viewed as larcenous behavior (for example, in hospitals, taking or eating hospital food without paying for it).

Items also were excluded if there was such restricted opportunity to commit the act that its inclusion would be meaningless (for example, taking money or cash in the hospital and manufacturing sectors).

Employing these selection criteria left us with the sector-specific employee-theft items presented in table 3-8. This table also combines the questionnaire responses from both phases of the research and presents the admitted levels of employee involvement for each theft item within each sector.

From an examination of table 3-8, we can see that the most prevalent theft item in the retail sector was the unauthorized use of the discount privilege, with 29 percent of the respondents reporting this act, 14 percent admitting involvement on four or more occasions within a year's time (that is, adding those who reported daily, once a week, or four to twelve times a year). The theft of property in the form of store merchandise was reported by nearly 7 percent of the retail respondents. Of the various items concerning the theft of money, the most prevalent was receiving pay for hours that were not worked. About 6 percent of the respondents reported involvement in this item. Directly borrowing or taking money from an employer without approval was reported by slightly less than 3 percent of the respondents.

In the hospital sector, the most reported theft item was the taking of hospital supplies, in which over 27 percent of the respondents reported involvement, 9 percent reporting four or more occurrences over the period of a year. In addition, almost 8 percent of the hospital respondents reported that they had taken medication intended for patients, 2 percent noting that this had happened on four or more occasions in a year. Five percent of the employees indicated that they had taken tools or equipment from the hospital, and approximately the same portion of hospital respondents as retail respondents (6 percent) reported being paid for hours not worked at least once a year.

In the manufacturing sector, the most reported theft item was the taking of raw materials used in the production process, with 14 percent of the respondents indicating that they had been involved in this form of theft. In contrast to the retail and hospital sectors, being paid for more hours than were worked was the second most prevalent item, with 9 percent of the respondents reporting involvement, over 3 percent admitting to four or more occurrences within a year. About 9 percent of the respondents reported taking company tools. A small portion (1.8 percent) reported taking precious metals. This percentage is noteworthy because of the significant value of these items when taken.

Table 3-8
Combined Phase I and Phase II Property-Deviance Items and Percentage of Reported Involvement, by Sector

		Involvement			
			Four to	One to	
		About	Twelve	Three	
	Almost	Once a	Times a	Times a	
Items	Daily	Week	Year	Year	Total
Retail Sector (N = 3,567)					
Misuse the discount privilege	0.6	2.4	11	14.9	28.9
Take store merchandise	0.2	0.5	1.3	4.6	6.6
Get paid for more hours than were worked	0.2	0.4	1.2	4	5.8
Purposely underring a purchase	0.1	0.3	1.1	1.7	3.2
Borrow or take money from employer without approval	0.1	0.1	0.5	2	2.7
Be reimbursed for more money than spent on business expenses	0.1	0.2	0.5	1.3	2.1
Damage merchandise to buy it on discount	—	0.1	0.2	1	1.3
Total involved in property deviance					35.1
Hospital Sector (N = 4,111)					
Take hospital supplies (for example, linens, bandages)	0.2	0.8	8.4	17.9	27.3
Take or use medication intended for patients	0.1	0.3	1.9	5.5	7.8
Get paid for more hours than were worked	0.2	0.5	1.6	3.8	6.1
Take hospital equipment or tools	0.1	0.1	0.4	4.1	4.7
Be reimbursed for more money than spent on business expenses	0.1	—	0.2	0.8	1.1
Total involved in property deviance					33.3
Manufacturing Sector (N = 1,497)					
Take raw materials used in production	0.1	0.3	3.5	10.4	14.3
Get paid for more hours than were worked	0.2	0.5	2.9	5.6	9.2
Take company tools or equipment	—	0.1	1.1	7.5	8.7
Be reimbursed for more money than spent on business expenses	0.1	0.6	1.4	5.6	7.7
Take finished products	—	—	0.4	2.7	3.1
Take precious metals (for example, platinum, gold)	0.1	0.1	0.5	1.1	1.8
Total involved in property deviance					28.4

The reader should note that the percentages of involvement for each of the theft items presented in table 3-8 cannot be added to equal the number of employees in each industry sector who reported some theft. Correspondingly, we have calculated the proportion of employees involved in at least some theft, however, and indicated this also in table 3-8. Due largely to the proportion of people reporting misuse of the discount privilege, over 35 percent of the 3,567 retail-store employees who completed questionnaires reported some involvement in the seven retail-theft items. In the hospital sector ($N = 4,111$), the percentage of those involved in at least some type of theft was approximately 33 percent. Last, in the manufacturing sector, 28 percent of the 1,497 respondents reported theft involvement in at least one of the six items included in the index. (Although these data do represent a significant level of activity in each of the three industry sectors, the reader is cautioned not be compare these figures directly because the number and type of theft items varied greatly from sector to sector.)

When various survey items are added together to make an index, the usual assumption is that the items are of equal weight—that is, indexes usually assume a direct additive quality of the included items. Considering that the previous examples of theft vary not only in seriousness but also in frequency of commission, an alternative to the simple additive index was necessary. In order to construct an employee-theft index within each sector, we had to represent each of the theft items as mathematically equivalent by transforming each item's raw scores into standard scores (or z scores), which have a mean of 0 and a standard deviation of 1. Thus, z-scores represent an individual's response to a deviance item in terms of the number of standard deviations from the average survey response. The advantage of using a technique like this is its greater sensitivity to the limited involvement in the more-serious theft items. For example, a score of almost daily involvement on a less-serious item (where the mean was also almost daily) would not overwhelm a score of one to three times on an item whose mean score was never. Standardizing each of the included theft items on its mean therefore allows us to add each of the items together, yielding a composite dependent-variable index equally representing the contribution of each measure of theft involvement.

Production-Deviance Dependent Variable

Since our theory of employee deviance suggests that we examine both employee theft and counterproductive behavior in our research, we also constructed an index of employee production-deviance behavior. The admitted levels of involvement for each of the production-deviance questionnaire items used to construct the index are presented in table 3-9. This table, which combines responses from Minneapolis-St. Paul, Dallas-Fort Worth, and Cleveland, allows us to examine identical counterproductive behaviors across the three industry sectors. (The reader should remember that data for the manufacturing sector were collected only in Phase I.) As we have already said, there was a difference in the level of involvement reported in Phase I and Phase II because of the time-frame differences in the two questionnaires. Thus, directly comparing the reported level of involvement in the manufacturing sector with the levels in the other two sectors must be done with caution.

The table does clearly show, however, that the most prevalent item in every sector was taking long lunches or breaks. In all three sectors, more than one-half of all respondents reported involvement in this activity. In the retail sector, the second most prevalent item was coming to work late or leaving early. Nearly one-third of the respondents reported being involved in this behavior. Two other items, using sick leave when not sick and doing slow or sloppy work, each were reported by over 15 percent of the retail respondents. Working under the influence of alcohol or drugs was the least prevalent item at 7.5 percent, although 3 percent indicated four or more occurrences in a year.

In the hospital sector, sick-leave misuse was the second most prevalent item, followed by coming to work late or leaving early. About 30 percent of the hospital respondents reported involvement in each activity. As among retail respondents, doing slow or sloppy work ranked fourth, and working under the influence of alcohol or drugs ranked fifth in reported prevalence. In the hospital sector, however, the percentage of respondents who reported working under the influence of alcohol or drugs was less than half as large as the percentage of retail respondents involved in the same activity.

In the manufacturing sector, coming late or leaving early was the second most prevalent item, and misuse of sick leave was third. About the same percentage of the manufacturing respondents reported being involved in each activity. Working under the influence of alcohol or drugs and doing slow or sloppy work were the least prevalent activities, with nearly the same percentage of respondents reporting involvement in each item.

As with the property-theft items, the percentages of involvement in table 3-9 cannot be directly added together. We have noted in the table the percentage of respondents in each sector who reported at least some involvement in any of the items used in the index of counterproductive activities. The figures clearly show that these activities were more prevalent than the theft items. In fact, production deviance was participated in by the majority of the respondents. Of the 3,567 retail respondents, 65 percent reported being involved in at least one of the five activities. Of the 4,111 employees in the hospital sector who returned questionnaries, 69 percent

Table 3-9
Combined Phase I and Phase II Production-Deviance Items and Percentage of Reported Involvement, by Sector

Items	Involvement				
	Almost Daily	About Once a Week	Four to Twelve Times a Year	One to Three Times a Year	Total
Retail Sector (N = 3,567)					
Take a long lunch or break without approval	6.9	13.3	15.5	20.3	56
Come to work late or leave early	0.9	3.4	10.8	17.2	32.3
Use sick leave when not sick	0.1	0.1	3.5	13.4	17.1
Do slow or sloppy work	0.3	1.5	4.1	9.8	15.7
Work under the influence of alcohol or drugs	0.5	0.8	1.6	4.6	7.5
Total involved in production deviance					65.4
Hospital Sector (N = 4,111)					
Take a long lunch or break without approval	8.5	13.5	17.4	17.8	57.2
Come to work late or leave early	1	3.5	9.6	14.9	29
Use sick leave when not sick	—	0.2	5.7	26.9	32.8
Do slow or sloppy work	0.2	0.8	4.1	5.9	11
Work under the influence of alcohol or drugs	0.1	0.3	0.6	2.2	3.2
Total involved in production deviance					69.2
Manufacturing Sector (N = 1,497)					
Take a long lunch or break without approval	18	23.5	22	8.5	72
Come to work late or leave early	1.9	9	19.4	13.8	44.1
Use sick leave when not sick	—	0.2	9.6	28.6	38.4
Do slow or sloppy work	0.5	1.3	5.7	5	12.5
Work under the influence of alcohol or drugs	1.1	1.3	3.1	7.3	12.8
Total involved in production deviance					82.2

indicated some involvement in the counterproductive-behavior items. In the manufacturing sector, 82 percent of the 1,497 respondents reported some involvement. (Again, the reader is cautioned not to make direct comparisons between the manufacturing sector and the retail and hospital sectors.)

Since the five questionnaire examples of production deviance, like property deviance, vary in seriousness and in frequency of occurrence, we again found it necessary to construct a scale. As with the property-theft items, with each sector we represented the production-deviance items as mathematically equivalent by transforming the raw scores into standardized scores. We subsequently summed the standardized scores for the five items within each sector to arrive at a dependent variable that equally takes into account each measure of counterproductive behavior.

Analysis Plan

In the following chapters we utilize correlation coefficients, multiple regression, and contingency tables to present our analysis of these data. For the latter, the dependent variables are dichotomized on the mean-scale score for each sector—that is, respondents who reported no deviance or less than average deviance are placed in the below-average category and are then compared with those scoring above the mean. This procedure is purposely conservative in that one could argue we should compare those respondents who have no involvement in employee deviance with those who have any involvement. However, we felt that such a division could distort our findings since it would include in the deviant category employees whose involvement was extremely low. With our procedure, we intend to determine whether respondents who reported a level of deviance above the average score for that particular industry sector are significantly different from employees whose involvement is below the average. In chapter 8, when we focus on organizations and organizational controls, we aggregate the individual-theft scores of each firm's respondents and obtain a mean theft score by company. This will allow us to compare the influence of different levels of organizational control on the reported prevalence of theft.

**Relationship between Property
and Production Deviance**

As we discussed in chapter 1, we collected data on both property and production deviance because we hypothesized the behaviors to be theoretically related. As a result of the self-report survey of employees, we are now able to demonstrate that relationship.

Table 3-10 indicates that in all three sectors the two dependent variables are correlated, with coefficients of .48 in retail, .45 in hospital, and .39 in manufacturing. These figures would suggest that those employees with higher levels of involvement in property theft may in fact also be more likely to participate in production deviance. Throughout our analysis to follow, we occasionally elaborate on the possible causal nature of the relationship between these two subcategories of employee deviance.

Employee Awareness of Deviance in the Organization

Although the face-to-face interviews conducted during Phase II with Minneapolis-St. Paul retail, hospital, and manufacturing employees were not specifically designed to provide us with an alternative measure of

Table 3-10
Pearson Product-Moment Correlations of Property Deviance with Production Deviance

	Property Deviance		
	Retail	Hospital	Manufacturing
Production Deviance	.48	.45	.39

Note: All coefficients are at the $p \leq .001$ level.

employee-deviance involvement, the interviews did confirm our basic findings about the prevalence of these behaviors.

As described in greater detail in chapter 2, during each interview the interviewee was asked to participate in a card-sort exercise. The employee was presented with approximately thirty cards that described property- or production-deviance activities associated with the interviewee's work environment. Included among these activities, which are listed in table 3-11, were the items of deviant behavior from each industry sector's self-administered questionnaire booklet, as well as additional items that were developed though a pretest of the procedure. Interviewees were asked to go through the set of cards and select those that they personally knew occurred in their organization. For the two corporations in each industry, this procedure provided us with a rough indication of employee awareness of property and production deviance.

In all three industry sectors, a high proportion of the interviewed employees reported that they were aware of production-deviance activities such as coming to work late or leaving early, using sick leave when not actually sick, coming to work under the influence of alcohol or drugs, and taking long lunches and coffee breaks. As one employee told an interviewer:

Taking longer lunch and/or coffee breaks: everybody's done it. [Retail sales clerk]

Moreover, employees from the three industries reported that these production-deviance activities occurred quite often. The phrase *pretty frequent* is an accurate reflection of how informants responded when asked about the frequency of these behaviors:

Longer breaks, I'd have to say that's pretty frequent. [Medical technologist]

Phrases such as *a lot of people do it* and *people do it all the time* were also given to explain how often these activities occur. Sometimes a specific

Table 3-11
Employee-Interview Property- and Production-Deviance Activities for Each Sector

Retail	Manufacturing	Hospital
1. Using sick leave when not sick	1. Using sick leave when not sick	1. Using sick leave when not sick
2. Getting paid for overtime not worked	2. Getting paid for overtime not worked	2. Getting paid for overtime not worked
3. Taking longer lunch and/or coffee breaks than authorized	3. Taking longer lunch and/or coffee breaks than authorized	3. Taking longer lunch and/or coffee breaks than authorized
4. Punching a time card for an absent employee	4. Punching a time card for an absent employee	4. Punching a time card for an absent employee
5. Coming late to work or leaving early without approval	5. Coming late to work or leaving early without approval	5. Coming late to work or leaving early without approval
6. Doing slow or sloppy work on purpose	6. Doing slow or sloppy work on purpose	6. Doing slow or sloppy work on purpose
7. Faking injury to receive workman's compensation	7. Faking inury to receive workman's compensation	7. Faking injury to receive workman's compensation
8. Using computer time for personal reasons or selling it to others	8. Using computer time for personal reasons or selling it to others	8. Using computer time for personal reasons or selling it to others
9. Working while under the influence of drugs or alcohol	9. Working while under the influence of drugs or alcohol	9. Working while under the influence of drugs or alcohol
10. Keeping samples	10. Keeping samples	10. Keeping samples
11. Taking and keeping personal property of co-workers	11. Taking and keeping personal property of co-workers	11. Taking and keeping personal property of co-workers
12. Taking care of personal business on company time	12. Taking care of personal business on company time	12. Taking care of personal business on company time
13. Actively helping another person take company property or merchandise	13. Actively helping another person take company property	13. Actively helping another person take hospital property
14. Giving away company property without the authority to do so	14. Giving away company property without the authority to do so	14. Giving away hospital property without the authority to do so
15. Falsifying a company document for personal gain	15. Falsifying a company document for personal gain	15. Falsifying a hospital document for personal gain
16. Using company copying machines for personal purposes	16. Using company copying machines for personal purposes	16. Using hospital copying machines for personal purposes
17. Making personal long-distance calls at company expense	17. Making personal long-distance calls at company expense	17. Making personal long-distance calls at hospital expense
18. Purposely mistreating or breaking company property	18. Purposely mistreating or breaking company property	18. Purposely mistreating or breaking hospital property

19. Using company tools or equipment for personal reasons away from the work place
20. Keeping company office supplies or equipment
21. Taking money from the company
22. Not reporting theft of company property by another employee
23. Disclosing confidential company documents or information for personal gain
24. Accepting money or gifts from competitors or clients
25. Taking company property that is of nominal value
26. Taking valuable company property or merchandise
27. Purposely damaging company merchandise so someone can buy it at a discount
28. Getting paid for more hours than scheduled
29. Underringing customer purchases for personal monetary gain
30. Using the discount privilege in an unauthorized manner

19. Using company tools or equipment for personal reasons away from the work place
20. Keeping company office supplies or equipment
21. Taking money from the company
22. Not reporting theft of company property by another employee
23. Disclosing confidential company documents or information for personal gain
24. Accepting money or gifts from clients
25. Deliberately sabotaging production
26. Taking valuable company property
27. Taking obsolete or defective parts or components, tools, or other types of equipment
28. Taking company property of little value

19. Using hospital tools or equipment for personal reasons away from the work place
20. Keeping hospital office supplies or equipment
21. Taking money from the hospital
22. Not reporting theft of hospital property by another employee
23. Disclosing confidential company documents or information for personal gain
24. Accepting money or gifts from sales representatives or patients
25. Taking or using medication intended for patients
26. Taking home hospital linen or other supplies
27. Taking home disposable patient supplies
28. Taking or eating hospital food without paying for it
29. Taking hospital supplies that are of nominal value
30. Taking and keeping a patient's property or money for personal use
31. Intentionally charging one patient for services or medication given to another

incident or type of occurrence was used to make an estimate of frequency. For example, the phrase *he's always loaded* is a graphic illustration of how an employee noticed others working under the influence of drugs or alcohol:

> There is one cleaning man that has such a drug problem—he's an alcoholic. He's always loaded. I do see that. [Nursing assistant]

Of the various property-deviance activities presented in the card sort, most retail employees were aware that the discount privilege was misused, and they indicated that this activity was widespread:

> When I started working there and everybody was giving discounts to their friends and stuff, it struck me because you can't give away discounts to everybody, but they said it's better than having them [the store] hold it [the item] and then you buy it for them [friends]. So I just figured . . . I can do it a couple of times, too. [Sales clerk]

Among hospital interviewees, activities under the general heading of "taking hospital supplies" were the most often selected property-deviance behaviors during the card sort. Employees reported that activities that would be included under this heading (for example, taking hospital linen or disposable patient supplies) occurred frequently:

> The example I thought of is [that] I know quite a few people have taken home uniforms and stuff like that. Use them as pajamas.
>
> *What's the scale of that? How much do you see?*
>
> It's not an unusual thing. [Orderly]

Of the property-deviance behaviors in the manufacturing sector, most employees were aware of the taking of raw materials used in production, and we were told that this was not an uncommon activity:

> The parts themselves—everybody wanted to take a part home, everybody in our line when they shut down second shift—everybody took a part home that cost over $185. Everybody goes by just to see what I've worked on, and so everybody took the part home to show everybody what they worked on and nobody would return it. That can hurt. Expecially when a part's $185 and there's, what, thirty of us in our line taking parts home. And there's first shift—about a hundred and some odd people on that line—and a lot of them have taken parts home. That's quite a bit of money that they've lost. [Assembler]

Fewer interviewed employees reported that they were aware of other property-deviance activities, and we were told that they occurred less frequently. For example, only a small number of hospital employees were aware of the item "taking and keeping a patient's property or money." When one employee who was aware of that activity was asked to cite an instance of that behavior, she referred to an incident several years past:

> We did have an employee once . . . this was a few years ago, that was just fired under Civil Service. There was a lighter missing, and it was a very unique lighter of a patient's property, and a nursing assistant . . . was found with it, had it at work right after. It was dumb. If somebody told you "I'm missing a lighter" and described it, you would remember it because it wasn't like this or anything like that. It probably wasn't worth that much. I mean how much can a lighter be worth unless it's gold or silver or something? He was caught right with the goods.
>
> *How long ago was that?*
>
> Oh, it has to be, I'd say, five years ago. [Nurse practitioner]

Similarly, in the retail sector, when asked about large-scale theft of merchandise or money, employees cited spectacular events that had received a great deal of attention in the organization (for example, $10,000 worth of merchandise stolen and $30,000 worth of merchandise purchased for a store by someone without the authority to do so).

> We've had a lady admit to stealing $4,000 worth of money and our garbage man had gotten fired, too, because he'd taken merchandise, put it in his bin, and taken it out to his car. He got out with $4,000 worth of merchandise he stole, too. [Sales clerk]
>
> One of the girls in the . . . department admitted to at least $500 in theft, and they think she probably took up to $5,000 worth. [Buyer]

The intensive interviews thus confirmed some of our general survey findings about the prevalence of property and production deviance. In addition, the interviews added to our knowledge about the prevalence of these activities by suggesting a reason for the differing prevalence of behaviors— namely, more discount misuse than other forms of property deviance in the retail sector; more production that property deviance in all three industries.

During the intensive interviews, employees consistently indicated that some of the activities included in the card sort would not always be defined by employees as deviant. Some employees could not draw the line between activities that go on and activities conventionally labeled theft or stealing. For example:

I know people copying for personal uses—copies of our weekly golf
schedule they hand out to the other golfers. That's sort of a personal thing,
but it's a company-sponsored thing. [Engineering manager]

The face-to-face employee interviews revealed the importance of
organizational and employee definitions of the situation within which acts
occur and are interpreted—that is, definitional processes within the work
place shaped informants' responses to items in the card-sort exercise. Some
acts were not perceived as deviant within certain contexts of the work setting. For example, taking longer breaks and taking certain items of nominal
value were found to be acceptable and normal patterns of employee
behavior within some work locations. This issue is discussed further in
chapter 10.

Conclusion

Our three data sources (the mail survey of employees, organizational interviews, and face-to-face employee interviews) gave us information about
employee deviance. Only the self-administered questionnaire survey of
employees, however, provided us with data to assess quantitatively the
prevalence of property and production deviance within the work place. The
following chapters utilize the two dependent variables constructed from the
survey data (property and production deviance) to test hypotheses about
the phenomenon of deviance by employees.

4 External Economic Pressures and Property Deviance

Perhaps the oldest and most pervasive of the available theories of employee theft concerns the effect of external economic pressures on the employee. As exemplified in Donald Cressey's work on embezzlers, the most consistent theme found was the employee who turned to theft as a solution to a financial bind, or what Cressey calls a "non-shareable problem."[1] Under extreme economic pressure, the employee violates his employer's trust and "borrows" from the company. While this theory has been applied most commonly to the study of cash embezzlers, the model has been utilized frequently to explain the phenomenon of employee theft as well. Not only would we expect the employee who is under a financial burden to steal cash, but also we would expect such an employee to be involved in all types of property theft that would be of direct financial benefit. Of course, this explanation assumes that materials stolen can be either converted to cash or directly applied to domestic economic needs.

The reader should realize that the self-administered questionnaire survey of employees was not designed to detect large-scale thefts of money, and for this and other reasons we cannot test exactly Cressey's non-shareable-problem hypothesis.[2] However, in this chapter we can test the validity of its property-theft corollary.

External economic pressures can operate at two levels: (1) the individual and (2) the social structural. On the individual level, we wished to examine whether those specific employees with economic difficulties were more involved in property deviance than their more financially secure peers. Specifically, the extent of financial pressure on individual survey respondents was determined by asking questions about their household income, the adequacy of that income, and their concern about their present financial situation. At the social-structural level, we wanted to know whether employees working in economically depressed communities were more prone to turn to crime as the innovative means to blocked economic goals.[3] This was measured by comparing the amounts of employee theft reported by respondents from two different communities in which we simultaneously collected data, Dallas-Fort Worth and Cleveland.

Personal Income

The employee survey presented respondents with ten different income ranges, varying from less than $5,000 to $50,000 or more. We asked

53

employees to indicate which range corresponded to their household's total yearly income.

The size of a family's income does not necessarily indicate the presence or absence of financial pressure. Circumstances arise that could cause a household with any income level to face occasional economic difficulties. However, if a family's annual income is extremely low, that family almost certainly will be under a financial strain due to the ever-increasing cost of living. For our examination of the variable family income, we predicted that, if financial pressures influence involvement in property theft, then individuals whose families subsisted on lower incomes were more likely to be involved.

In table 4-1 we see that in no industry sector did we confirm the predicted hypothesis. In the retail sector the relationship between family income and employee-theft involvement was bimodal—that is, respondents who were more likely to be involved in theft came from families with very low incomes (under $5,000) as well as from households where the annual income exceeded $20,000. In the hospital sector, we found a significant relationship between income level and theft involvement, but the results were counter to those that had been predicted in that respondents from higher-income families were more likely to be involved. In the manufacturing sec-

Table 4-1
Employee Theft, by Household Income of Respondent

	Retail Sector			Employee Theft Hospital Sector			Manufacturing Sector		
Income	*Percent Below Mean*	*Percent Above Mean*	*N*	*Percent Below Mean*	*Percent Above Mean*	*N*	*Percent Below Mean*	*Percent Above Mean*	*N*
Less than $5,000	69.4	30.6	108	74.7	25.3	87	75	25	8
$5,000 to $9,999	83.5	16.5	340	73.3	26.7	382	85.5	14.5	62
$10,000 to $14,999	80.8	19.2	447	67.9	32.1	695	72.6	27.4	179
$15,000 to $19,999	80	20	486	67.2	32.8	680	68	32	231
$20,000 to $24,999	74.1	25.9	599	65.9	34.1	704	70	30	357
$25,000 to $29,999	72.4	27.6	431	63.2	36.8	527	71.7	28.3	269
$30,000 to $34,999	75.2	24.8	331	62.6	37.4	364	70	30	170
$35,000 to $39,999	75.8	24.2	223	68.1	31.9	191	73.4	26.6	94
$40,000 to $49,999	64.9	35.1	211	61.7	38.3	193	71.2	28.8	66
$50,000 or more	72.9	27.1	214	63.8	36.2	174	75	25	44
Total	76	24	3,390	66.5	33.5	3,997	71.4	28.6	1,480
	$X^2 = 42.66$, 9 df; $p \leq .000$ Gamma $= .119$			$X^2 = 19.30$, 9 df; $p \leq .023$ Gamma $= .082$			$X^2 = 8.52$, 9 df; $p = $ NS Gamma $= .016$		

tor, table 4-1 shows the relationship between family income and theft to be curvilinear. Higher levels of theft were reported by manufacturing employees whose families earned between $15,000 and $35,000 per year. In sum, when using household income as a measure of economic need, we found no consistent evidence to support the hypothesis that financial resources motivate an individual to become involved in property deviance at work.

The fact that we discerned a somewhat puzzling set of relationships between family income and employee theft in each sector could be due to the differing natures of the three particular industries surveyed and their work forces. For example, the bipolar relationship in the retail sector might be explained by the relatively low wage scale of the industry and its heavy reliance on student workers who live with their parents. In hospitals, conversely, the greater involvement of employees from higher-income families might reflect the fact that higher-status professionals comprise a large portion of that industry's work force. In sum, our analysis of household income suggests that occupational and personal characteristics of employees might be the more-important variables to understand employee involvement in deviant behavior. These alternative variables are discussed in later chapters.

Income Adequacy

To ascertain the adequacy of a family's income, we asked each respondent to indicate whether the household's income was sufficient to meet the usual bills and expenses. The possible response choices to this question in the Minneapolis-St. Paul (Phase I) survey were always, usually, and never. Since the majority of the respondents answered "usually," we felt that we inadvertently had constrained the variance on this question. Therefore, for the second phase of the research in Dallas-Fort Worth and Cleveland, we added an extra category of seldom between usually and never. In examining this variable, we predicted that a person whose income was never sufficient would be under more economic pressure than one who could always meet expenses. If economic pressure influences involvement in property theft, the employee respondents who answered "never" should be more involved.

Since the response choices for this question differed slightly between the Minneapolis-St. Paul study and the research in Dallas-Fort Worth and Cleveland, our analysis treated respondents from each phase separately. Table 4-2 presents two retail-sector contingency tables, table 4-3 contains two cross-tabulations for the hospital sector, and table 4-4 shows cross-tabulations for manufacturing in the Twin Cities. These tables show that the relationship between property-deviance involvement and income ade-

Table 4-2
Employee Theft, by the Adequacy of the Respondent's Income,
in the Retail Sector

Income Adequacy	Percent Below Mean	Percent Above Mean	N
	Minneapolis-St. Paul		
Always	60	40	505
Usually	67.2	32.8	756
Never	71.3	28.7	122
Total	64.9	35.1	1,383

$X^2 = 9.28$, 2 df; $p \leq .010$
Gamma $= -.156$

Income Adequacy	Percent Below Mean	Percent Above Mean	N
	Dallas-Fort Worth and Cleveland		
Always	83.2	16.8	560
Usually	83.4	16.6	1,103
Seldom	82.2	17.8	320
Never	83.1	16.9	148
Total	83.2	16.8	2,131

$X^2 = .27$, 3 df; $p = $ NS
Gamma $= .013$

quacy was nonsignificant in the hospital sector for Minneapolis-St. Paul and in the retail sectors for Dallas-Fort Worth and Cleveland. Alternatively, in the retail and manufacturing sectors in Minneapolis-St. Paul and the hospital industry in Dallas-Fort Worth and Cleveland, the results were significant but opposite of what was predicted—that is, in four instances the data show that respondents who reported their incomes as "never sufficient" were less likely to be involved in theft. In conclusion, we can safely say that this variable provided us with no clear evidence that overwhelming economic burdens were pushing individuals into work-place property-deviance involvement.

Financial Concern

The third variable of interest from the employee survey was obtained by asking respondents to indicate how concerned they were about their current financial situation. We presented every respondent with eight issues of possible interest: (1) personal health, (2) neighborhood crime, (3) family

Table 4-3
**Employee Theft, by the Adequacy of the Respondent's Income,
in the Hospital Sector**

Income Adequacy	Employee Theft		
	Percent Below Mean	Percent Above Mean	N
Minneapolis-St. Paul			
Always	68.2	31.8	730
Usually	67	33	1,162
Never	70	30	160
Total	67.7	32.3	2,052

$X^2 = .71$, 2 df; p = NS
Gamma = .005

Dallas-Fort Worth and Cleveland			
Always	58.9	41.1	475
Usually	63.1	36.9	1,069
Seldom	73.6	26.4	311
Never	88.2	11.8	153
Total	65.7	34.3	2,008

$X^2 = 55.87$, 3 df; $p \leq .001$
Gamma = −.260

welfare, (4) pollution, (5) present job, (6) religion, (7) financial situation, and (8) education/career traininig. We asked the respondents to rank these issues from one through eight, based upon the order of their personal importance to the respondent.

Being concerned about finances and being under financial pressure are not necessarily the same. However, if a respondent considered his or her finances as one of the most important issues, that concern could be partially due to "unshareable economic problems,"[4] or it could also be that current realities are not matching one's financial aspirations regardless of the income presently being realized. Either way, we predicted higher levels of involvement in employee theft among respondents who were highly concerned about their financial situations, independent of actual income level.

The results of this analysis, shown in table 4-5, indicate that the relationship between property deviance and financial concern is at least consistent across all three sectors. In each industry, the results are significant, with higher-theft individuals more likely to be concerned about their finances, particularly those who ranked finances as the first or second most important issue. These relationships are as we predicted.

Table 4-4
Employee Theft, by the Adequacy of the Respondent's Income, in the Manufacturing Sector

| Income Adequacy | Employee Theft | | N |
	Percent Below Mean	Percent Above Mean	
Always	70.3	29.7	508
Usually	69.8	30.2	839
Never	86.7	13.3	143
Total	71.6	28.4	1,490

$X^2 = 17.78$, 2 df; $p \leq .001$
Gamma $= -.123$

This analysis suggests that an individual's financial situation may indeed play a part in influencing theft involvement. However, when all three of the variables presented here are considered, it appears that financial pressures perceived by an individual may not be among the best predictors of employee involvement in property deviance.

Community Pressures

In addition to the measures of economic pressure provided by responses to the employee survey, we hypothesized that yet another source of employee-deviance pressure may be provided by the financial and behavioral climate present in one's community—that is, the economic situation within the community in which an individual lives and works could affect that person's financial viability and hence influence his or her decision to become involved in employee theft.

Since we simultaneously surveyed employees in Dallas-Fort Worth and Cleveland, we were afforded a unique opportunity to compare the amounts of theft reported by respondents from two different communities. As noted in chapter 2, we specifically included Dallas-Fort Worth and Cleveland in the second phase of the research because of their differing official crime and victimization survey rates. We wanted to see if the level of observed crime in the community would be reflected in the amount of employee theft in the work place—specifically, Dallas-Fort Worth, high larceny; Cleveland, low larceny.

Along with having different rates of crime, however, the two metropolitan areas are also economically distinct. On the one hand,

Table 4-5
Employee Theft, by the Respondent's Concern with Personal Finances

Rank of Financial Situation as a Concern	Retail Sector			Hospital Sector			Manufacturing Sector		
	Percent Below Mean	Percent Above Mean	N	Percent Below Mean	Percent Above Mean	N	Percent Below Mean	Percent Above Mean	N
First	70.9	29.1	244	58.3	41.7	218	61.7	38.3	94
Second	72.1	27.9	587	64	36	550	64.6	35.4	268
Third	76.2	23.8	881	65.1	34.9	1,025	72.6	27.4	441
Fourth	75.7	24.3	837	63.1	36.9	1,007	73.1	26.9	361
Fifth	80.1	19.9	544	70.5	29.5	638	74	26	196
Sixth	78.5	21.5	200	76.2	23.8	336	77.8	22.2	63
Seventh	74.3	25.7	101	70.2	29.8	121	81.5	18.5	27
Eighth	68.6	31.4	35	72.2	27.8	54	100	—	13
Total	75.6	24.4	3,429	66.1	33.9	3,949	71.4	28.6	1,463

$X^2 = 15.12$, 7 df; $p \leq .035$ Gamma $= -.080$ $X^2 = 34.41$, 7 df; $p \leq .000$ Gamma $= -.106$ $X^2 = 19.73$, 7 df; $p \leq .006$ Gamma $= -.152$

Cleveland is an example of a northern industrial city that is losing both population and industry. Between 1970 and 1980, the population declined 8 percent,[5] and during the four-month period in 1980 when these data were collected, the unemployment rate in the Cleveland community averaged 8.2 percent.[6] Dallas-Fort Worth, on the other hand, is the epitome of the booming sun-belt city. Both the population and economy are expanding; the population increased 25.1 percent from 1970 to 1980.[7] In contrast to Cleveland, the Dallas-Forth Worth unemployment rate during the survey period in 1980 averaged 4.6 percent.[8]

From a theoretical standpoint, hypothesizing exactly how the economic situation in a community would affect employee-theft involvement is uncertain. In a city like Cleveland that has high unemployment, the state of the economy could lead to increased crime among all members of the population. However, among employed individuals, the poor economic situation might lead to lesser amounts of employee theft—that is, with fewer jobs available people might not want to run the risk of stealing, getting caught, and subsequently losing their jobs.

In Dallas-Fort Worth, a healthy economy and full employment could be expected to yield a period of lower property theft in the work place. However, relatively low unemployment might also lead an individual to have less fear of losing his or her job since a person terminated for involvement in theft could most likely find immediate employment with another

organization. Since the economic situation could variously affect theft by
employees, we could not predict which of the two communities was more
likely to have higher amounts of reported theft involvement.

From table 4-6 we see that, in the retail sector, respondents from
Cleveland were slightly more likely to be involved in employee theft [with a
weak Yule's Q (gamma) of .13], while the relationship between the two
cities in the hospital sector was nonsignificant.

Since we received slightly different results for the two sectors, we
wanted to be certain that the marginally significant relationship in the retail
sector was real and not the result of the varying characteristics of the
specific retail organizations included in the study. In the retail sector, two
separate technologies are represented: full-line department stores and discount stores. Department stores carry somewhat different lines of merchandise than discounters, and employees in a department store are engaged in
different work activities than their counterparts in a discount operation.
Therefore, to be certain that we obtained an accurate picture of the influence attributable to a local community's economy upon employee theft,
we dropped the two discount stores in the sample and then retested for community differences only among the full-line department stores. As we see in
table 4-7, when we controlled for store technology, there was no significant
relationship among similar retailing organizations. Therefore, we have to
conclude that our data do not provide sufficient evidence to support the
hypothesis that community differences regarding economy or crime rates
affect an individual employee's involvement in theft.

Conclusion

From our examination of various measures of an individual employee's
perceived economic difficulties, we found very little evidence to support the

Table 4-6
Employee Theft, by Community

	Employee Theft					
	Retail Sector			Hospital Sector		
Community	Percent Below Mean	Percent Above Mean	N	Percent Below Mean	Percent Above Mean	N
Dallas-Fort Worth	77.6	22.4	1,322	66.4	33.6	920
Cleveland	72.8	27.2	837	65.3	34.7	1,111
Total	75.7	24.3	2,159	65.8	34.2	2,031
	$X^2 = 6.30$, 1 df; $p \leq .012$ Yule's Q = .130			$X^2 = .21$, 1 df; $p =$ NS Yule's Q = .024		

Table 4-7
Employee Theft, by Community, in Full-Line Department Stores

	Employee Theft		
Community	Percent Below Mean	Percent Above Mean	N
Dallas-Fort Worth	84.6	15.4	1,085
Cleveland	81.8	18.2	710
Total	83.5	16.5	1,795

$$X^2 = 2.21, 1 \text{ df}; p = NS$$
$$\text{Yule's Q} = .099$$

hypothesis that employees become involved in theft because of greater economic pressure. Indeed, there may be a pool of people who turn to employee theft to solve economic difficulties, but these data suggest that this variable probably predicts employee-theft involvement for a small number of individuals.

We also considered the economic situation of the community as an indicator of employee-theft behavior. However, we found no significant influence. The only relationship that appeared from the analysis was attributable to the differing technologies of the surveyed organizations rather than the community. The overall results presented in this chapter thus suggest that factors external to the organization are neither the best nor the most consistent predictors of employee involvement in work-place property deviance. Therefore, in succeeding chapters we direct our attention to those factors internal to the work organization for explanations of the phenomenon of employee theft.[9]

Notes

1. Donald Cressey, *Other People's Money: A Study in the Social Psychology of Embezzlement* (Belmont, Calif.: Wadsworth, 1953).

2. Ibid.

3. R.K. Merton, "Social Structure and Anomie," *American Sociological Review* 3 (1938):672-682.

4. Cressey, *Other People's Money*.

5. U.S. Bureau of Census, *Statistical Abstract of the United States: 1981*, 102d ed. (Washington, D.C.: Government Printing Office, 1981), p. 18.

6. U.S. Department of Labor, Employment and Training Administration, *Area Trends in Employment and Unemployment: January-June 1981* (Washington, D.C.: Government Printing Office, 1981), p. 57.

7. Bureau of Census, *Statistical Abstract*.

8. Department of Labor, *Area Trends*, p. 61.

9. D.L. Altheide et al., "The Social Meanings of Employee Theft," in *Crime at the Top*, eds. J.M. Johnson and J.D. Douglas (Philadelphia: Lippincott, 1978), pp. 90-124.

5

Youth, Work, and Property Deviance

One of the more-perplexing research and policy questions that has arisen from the analysis of apprehended employee thieves is the disproportionately higher number of younger workers found involved in theft activity. One recent analysis of a major Midwest retail department store's theft records indicated that although the 18-to-22-year-old age group made up only 12 percent of the total work force, it accounted for 69 percent of the violations for employee theft.[1] Further, Franklin observed that 62 percent of the employees apprehended for theft were unmarried.[2] A similar retail study conducted ten years earlier found that 33 percent of those employees detected for involvement in theft were with the company less than six months and that almost two-thirds were employed less than two years.[3] These statistics, if correct, paint a very bleak portrait of young, single, short-tenured employees and their involvement in deviance, particularly theft. Their image is so tainted that one author, writing in an industry trade journal, warns that the "part-time, teenage" employee is the single greatest business-theft threat.[4]

This chapter examines the self-report data from the earlier chapters in an attempt either to confirm or reject these pessimistic official statistics on youth and theft. Additionally, if these data do verify the negative relationship between age and theft involvement, what causal hypotheses might we use to explain the inordinately high level of deviance involvement among such a large number of employees who are just beginning their employment careers?

Age and Property Deviance

Few other variables in this book have exhibited such a strong relationship to theft as the age of the employee. As tables 5-1, 5-2, and 5-3 show, there seems to be little doubt that the official statistics compiled from employees apprehended for theft are an accurate reflection of the true theft picture. Among our three industry sectors, retail, hospital and manufacturing, we found zero-order correlation coefficients of $-.26$, $-.19$, and $-.17$ respectively. Younger employees did seem to report higher theft levels than their older peers. The critical question seems to be Why?

The numerical age of an individual by itself is not a social variable. The negative correlations found between age and employee-theft involvement have little theoretical meaning unless we can understand their sociological

Table 5-1

Employee Age, Its Covariants, and Property-Theft Involvement in the Retail Sector

	Property Theft	Marital Status	Concern with Education/Career	Looking for a New Job	Tenure with Company	Age
Property Theft	1.0					
Marital Status	.18[a] (.08)	1.0				
Concern with Education/Career	.21 (.06)	.44	1.0			
Looking for a New Job	−.17 (−.07)	−.27	−.34	1.0		
Tenure with Company	−.14 (.02)	−.25	−.41	.34	1.0	
Age	−.26	−.44	−.63	.45	.62	1.0

[a]All coefficients at the $p \leq .001$ level. (Coefficients with age controlled in parentheses.)

underpinnings. For example, an individual's age has implications for one's physical, psychological, and social development. In addition, age is highly correlated with structural variables present in society (in this case, the work setting), such as tenure, wage, and occupational status. Thus, to appreciate better the social effects of age, it is necessary to review the theoretical models explaining the disproportionately higher involvement levels of younger employees in acts of theft agains the work organization.

One commonly expressed theoretical model states that younger employees just are not as honest or ethical as those of previous generations.

Table 5-2

Employee Age, Its Covariants, and Property-Theft Involvement in the Hospital Sector

	Property Theft	Marital Status	Concern with Education/Career	Looking for a New Job	Tenure with Company	Age
Property Theft	1.0					
Marital Status	.07[a] (.05)	1.0				
Concern with Education/Career	.16 (.09)	.18	1.0			
Looking for a New Job	−.11 (−.06)	−.13	−.22	1.0		
Tenure with Company	−.12 (.00)	−.08	−.30	.26	1.0	
Age	−.19	−.15	−.40	.31	.63	1.0

[a]All coefficients significant at the $p \leq .001$ level. (Coefficients with age controlled in parentheses.)

Table 5-3
Employee Age, Its Covariants, and Property-Theft Involvement in the Manufacturing Sector

	Property Theft	Marital Status	Concern with Education/Career	Looking for a New Job	Tenure with Company	Age
Property Theft	1.0					
Marital Status	.07[a] (.03)	1.0				
Concern with Education/Career	.09 (.02)	.26	1.0			
Looking for a New Job	−.06 (−.02)	−.12	−.22	1.0		
Tenure with Company	−.05 (.08)	−.21	−.28	.25	1.0	
Age	−.17	−.26	−.40	.26	.65	1.0

[a]All coefficients at the $p \leq .001$ level. (Coefficients with age controlled in parentheses.)

Advocates of this theory point to the official retail-theft statistics presented earlier and conclude that significant generational differences exist among today's younger work force. The further implication from this model is that these higher levels of employee deviance and theft will only increase as greater numbers of this less-ethical generation of employees enter the work force. Unfortunately, our self-report survey does not provide the kind of longitudinal data necessary to test this intergenerational-integrity hypothesis. Perhaps when and if this work is replicated in the same companies some years from now it might be possible to determine the validity of this model.

We do, however, have data to evaluate a competing hypothesis regarding the relationship between age and theft. Fortunately, if correct, this model offers a less-gloomy picture of the future regarding employee theft and the younger employee. Specifically, we posit that higher levels of theft among younger employees may simply be a function of lesser commitment to the organization, combined with lesser social risk to those employees actually involved in the theft behavior. This model holds that employee theft always has and always will be greater among younger, unmarried, short-tenured workers. Accordingly, the retail industry has noticed the higher theft involvement of younger employees due to the greater reliance of retailers upon these workers, especially during the peak Christmas holiday sales period.

Age and Property Deviance with Control Variables

In order to understand better the social meaning of this lesser-commitment/lesser-risk hypothesis, we have included in the following sections an empirical examination of four variables that are covariant with age (see tables 5-1, 5-2, and 5-3).

Tenure

When we compared the number of months employed to self-reported prevalence of theft involvement, a significant negative relationship was observed for workers in all three sectors (retail, $r = -.14$; hospitals, $r = -.12$; and manufacturing, $r = -.05$). However, when the age of the employee was controlled (coefficients included in parentheses), this relationship all but disappeared among retail and hospital employees and became positive in manufacturing. Thus, we conclude that those with little tenure with the organization who were more involved in theft were also more likely to be younger employees.

Concern about Education/Career

Each respondent was asked to rank order eight concerns, ranging from one's health, crime in the neighborhood, pollution, family welfare, and religion to those more directly related to job, financial situation, and education/career training. Only one of these concerns consistently predicted theft involvement—namely, concern about one's education and career. As with tenure, when we controlled by age the relationship lessened dramatically in all three industry sectors, indicating that this trait is most commonly held by the younger members of the work force. To these employees, the present job may be a temporary means of earning money until the goal of educational training is achieved.

Looking for a Job

Although we also include this variable in chapter 7 (which discusses job dissatisfaction and theft), the fact that an employee anticipates leaving his or her present job to look for another is an indirect measure of minimal commitment to a work organization. In all three sectors (retail, $r = -.17$; hospitals, $r = -.11$; and manufacturing, $r = -.06$, we found statistically significant negative correlation coefficients with theft behavior for those employees who were looking for a new job. Controlling by age reduced each of these three coefficients by more than half. Again, we observe that more often it was the younger employee who had intentions of moving on to a different employment experience, perhaps even to a career obtained by completing the aforementioned educational program.

Marital Status

Marital status for both sexes can be utilized as an indirect measure of organizational commitment and social risk. In all three industry sectors, especially retail ($r = .18$), we found that unmarried employees were more likely to be involved in theft activity against the work organization. We expect that unmarried employees may be more occupationally mobile and also be at less-serious economic risk if detected for theft activity. Further, we would predict that the threat of being detected and terminated for theft activity would be much less salient to the employee without a spouse or family depending on the employee's income. As expected, when we controlled by age we found that these unmarried employees were much more likely to be concentrated in the younger age groups.

Conclusion

Although we do not have longitudinal survey data to evaluate adequately the moral or ethical intergenerational-integrity hypothesis, these data did strongly support our alternative theoretical model suggesting that many younger employees are simply less socially and emotionally committed to their present place of work and are also under less social risk if detected. We found that the younger employees who reported higher involvement in theft were more likely to have very little tenure with the organization. Further, they indicated greater personal concern with their current educational and career training than with their present jobs. In addition, they were the employees who were more likely to be looking for a new job in the coming year. Finally, many of the employees who were more likely to be involved in theft activity were unmarried and, therefore, without the associated financial responsibilities.

In summary, we found that the employees who had lower levels of commitment to their present work organization reported higher levels of theft activity. By definition, these employees are also more likely to be younger workers. There is an existing theoretical explanation for this finding in the criminological literature that may help us to understand this phenomenon. A juvenile-delinquency theory (which has later come to be incorporated in control theory), posited first by Briar and Piliavin in 1965, works remarkably well in understanding the higher level of deviance by the younger worker.[5] These authors propose that the central process of social control is determined by one's "commitment to conformity."[6] According to this model; assuming that all employees are subject to relatively the same deviant motives and opportunities, the probability of deviant involvement will be dependent upon the stakes that one has invested in conformity. In subsequent empirical tests of this social-control model, both Piliavin and his associates and Hirschi demonstrate the importance of understanding the rewards (or stakes) that a deviant employee places in jeopardy while committing rule-breaking behavior.[7] Thus, in the employment setting the younger employee clearly has much less to lose than his older co-worker if apprehended and punished for theft.

The policy implications derived from these findings may be more related to the way in which these marginal employees are treated by the organization than to their moral or ethical inclinations. If we accept the proposed stakes-in-conformity explanation, the traditional organizational view of the younger employee should be modified extensively, especially in those industries that have large proportions of younger workers, such as retailing and hospitals. Rather than treating these younger employees as threats to the work organization, companies should afford younger workers many of the same rights, fringes, and privileges of the tenured, older employees. In fact, by signaling to the younger employee that he or she is temporary or expendable, the organization inadvertently may be encouraging its own victimization by the very group of employees that is already least committed to the expressed goals and objectives of the owners and managers.

Notes

1. Alice Pickett Franklin, *Internal Theft in a Retail Organization: A Case Study* (Ann Arbor, Mich.: University Microfilms, 1975).
2. Ibid.
3. G. Robin, "Employees as Offenders," *Journal of Research on Crime and Delinquency* 6 (1969):17-33.
4. L.E. Daykin, "Employee Theft—It Hurts the Worst," *Progressive Grocer* 49 (November 1970):42-48, 50, 52.
5. Scott Briar and Irving Piliavin, "Delinquency, Situational Inducements, and Commitment to Conformity," *Social Problems* 13 (1965):35-45.
6. Ibid., p. 39.
7. Irving M. Piliavin, Arlene C. Vadum, and Jane Allyn Hardyck, "Delinquency, Personal Costs and Parental Treatment: A Test of the Reward-Cost Model of Juvenile Criminality," *Journal of Criminal Law, Criminology and Police Science* 60 (1969):165-172; and Travis Hirschi, *Causes of Delinquency* (Berkeley: University of California Press, 1969).

6 Opportunity, Occupation, and Employee Deviance

One of the most commonly expressed theories of employee theft and counter-productive activity is predicated on the supposition that the opportunity to indulge in such acts is the key factor to understanding deviant employee behavior. Many industrial-security practitioners maintain that all employees have larcenous tendencies and that, if given the chance, they will take or abuse the property and other assets of their employers. Followers of this theoretical model advise that the most efficient method of reducing theft in the work place is to bolt everything down and to watch everyone—that is, drastically curtail the opportunity for theft, thereby reducing the temptation to steal. Of course, this line of thought deals only with differential access to materials and does not directly address differential exposure to or involvement in social structures that tend to support deviant behavior.[1]

Individuals who advocate an opportunity theory of employee deviance usually accompany their pessimistic warnings with various suggestions by which an organization can minimize losses.[2] These changes typically are directed toward tightening organizational security and personnel, financial, and inventory controls. The relationship between these various formal organizational controls and the level of employee-theft involvement is an important and complex one, meriting a separate treatment in chapter 8. In this chapter, however, we focus more carefully on a basic premise of the opportunity hypothesis—namely, that the prevalence of theft and deviance throughout an organization varies by occupation or job title.

In the corporate work world, an underlying perspective of opportunity theory maintains that an employee's ability to engage in theft is constrained by his or her occupational position in the company. Specifically, an employee's direct contact with and knowledge about those things to be taken should correlate with theft-involvement levels. For example, a person holding a job as a cashier would be in contact with cash and would know the systems for reporting overcharges and underrings. Persons holding other occupations in an organization could have more-restricted access to money and might not know the procedures used to account for such cash transactions.

Measurement

The self-administered questionnaire survey provided us with information on the general occupational titles of employee respondents. In each sector, respondents were presented with a list of approximately thirty jobs usually found in the respondent's industry sector (hospital, retail department stores, and manufacturing). We asked each employee to indicate the occupational category that best described his or her current job. To test our opportunity hypothesis, we compared the average amounts of property and production deviance reported by respondents in each of the major occupational categories.

The reader should note that some of the items included in the property-deviance dependent variable were not equally applicable to all employees. For example, the ability to be reimbursed for more money than actually spent on business expenses was limited to those persons who had expense accounts. Differences in applicability could lead to more theft being reported by people in some occupations than others. However, given the variety of activities included in the dependent variable, we feel it can be used to give us an indication of differential occupational involvement.

Occupational Title and Property Deviance

Figures 6-1, 6-2 and 6-3 present the average levels of property theft reported by each occupational category in the retail, hospital, and manufacturing sectors respectively. The figures also indicate the number of sampled respondents representing each category. To facilitate presentation of the data, each sector's occupations are divided into four subgroups based upon occupational-status rankings as utilized by the U.S. Bureau of the Census.

These figures consistently show that within each industry, the theoretically predicted sets of occupational categories report above-average levels of property deviance. As expected, within each industry sector, the occupational categories with higher average levels of theft tended to involve close and/or unrestricted access to materials or money. Sales clerks, stockroom workers, and buyers in retail stores are in daily contact with store merchandise, and sales clerks and cashiers work with cash. In the hospital sector, most of the above-average theft occupations were patient-care-ward-related jobs. Registered nurses, residents, physicians, technologists, therapists, and nursing assistants use hospital supplies when caring for patients on a day-to-day basis. In the manufacturing sector, the majority of the occupations that reported an above-average level of theft were professional or technical occupations (mechanical and electrical engineers, computer specialists, technicians), occupations normally involving unrestricted access to tools, raw materials, and finished products. The figures tend to confirm that an employee's involvement in theft may be related to the physical opportunities furnished by his or her occupation.

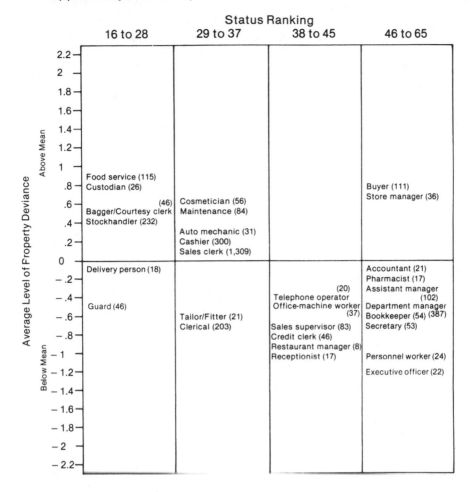

Figure 6-1. Average Level of Property Deviance for Each Occupational
Classification, Retail Sector

Occupational Title and Production Deviance

We also computed the production-deviance averages reported by each occupation. From figure 6-4 we can see that in the retail sector most of the occupational groups that had above-mean levels of property deviance also
reported higher amounts of production deviance (sales clerks, buyers,
cashiers, stock handlers). For the manufacturing sector (figure 6-6), a
similar situation is evident, in that people holding professional or the
technical occupations reported above-average involvement both in property
and production deviance. Figure 6-5 for the hospital sector, however, shows

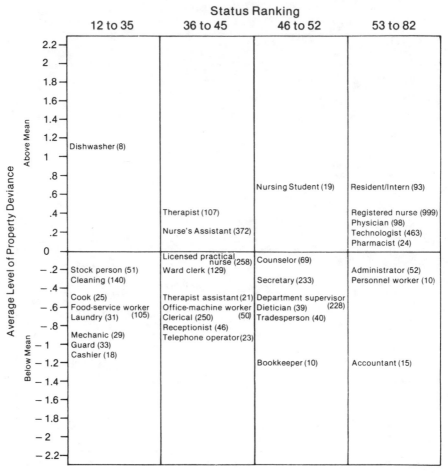

Figure 6-2. Average Level of Property Deviance for Each Occupational Classification, Hospital Sector

that occupations with above-mean levels of production deviance differed from those with above-average property deviance; that is, some of the primary patient-ward occupations with high levels of property theft (registered nurses, nursing students, residents, and physicians) reported below-average levels of production deviance, possibly because of the greater personal commitment to the patient that is characteristic of these more-professionalized occupations.

Conclusion

Not surprisingly, at first glance our data suggest that the highest theft occupational categories in all three industry sectors are those positions with

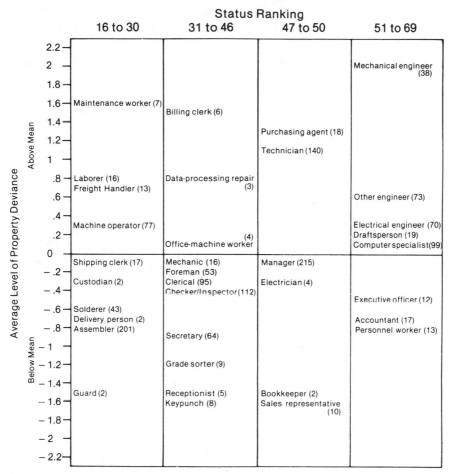

Figure 6-3. Average Level of Property Deviance for Each Occupational Classification, Manufacturing Sector

almost unrestricted access to the things of value in the work organization. However, this observation was not without its industry-specific qualifications. In short, the fact that the high-opportunity/high-theft hypothesis seemed to operate differently in each industry sector examined shortly implies that our opportunity hypothesis is not as simple as we have predicted.

The retail sample conforms most closely to our hypothesized relationship to employee theft—namely, the most theft was reported by those occupational categories with the greatest access and least social status in the work organization. Since the things to be taken in a retail store have great desirability across all employee levels, we did find the highest theft levels among those employee categories who handle cash and merchandise on a daily basis.

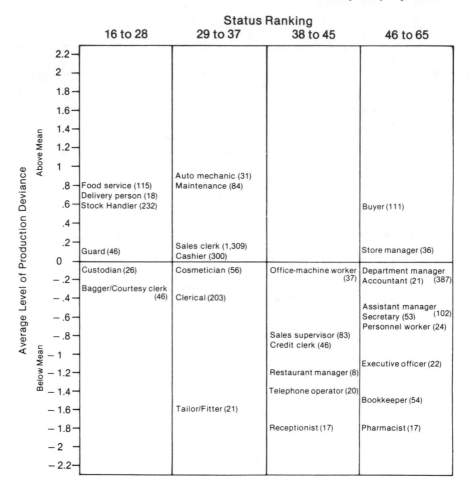

Figure 6-4. Average Level of Production Deviance for Each Occupational
           Classification, Retail Sector

Before we immediately confirm the direct effect of opportunity, let us
examine two contradictory additional findings. First, when we also examined production deviance by occupational category, we found almost exactly the same job-title groupings. Since production deviance is more equally
possible among all retail occupations, this suggests that opportunity is not
the only variable operating here. Second, we note that in retail the high
property- and production-deviance categories (with the exception of buyers
and store managers) are clustered in the lower-social-status occupational
categories. While we cannot dismiss the effect of opportunity in retail, it
seems quite likely that another variable may be correlated to both occupa-

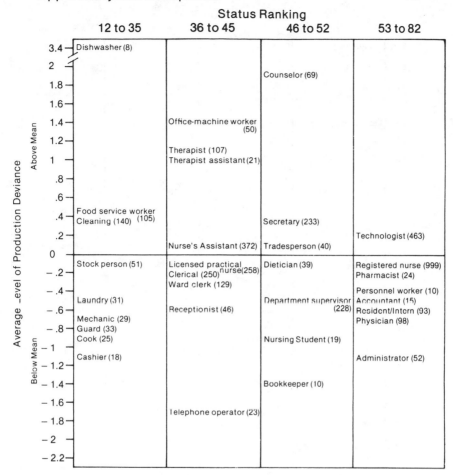

Figure 6-5. Average Level of Production Deviance for Each Occupational Classification, Hospital Sector

tion and theft, giving us a spurious relationship. That variable might be job dissatisfaction, which we discuss in the next chapter. In manufacturing we found a pattern different from retail: The high-theft employees seemed to be grouped among the high-status engineering and technical employees. In fact, the low-status assembly-line personnel—assumedly those with the greatest direct access to the company's property—as a group reported one of the lowest levels of theft. This finding strongly suggests that it is not simply access that is important here. Among manufacturing employees, knowledge about the things to be taken or nature of the control environment also seems to be critical to understanding the effect of opportunity, as we shall see later.

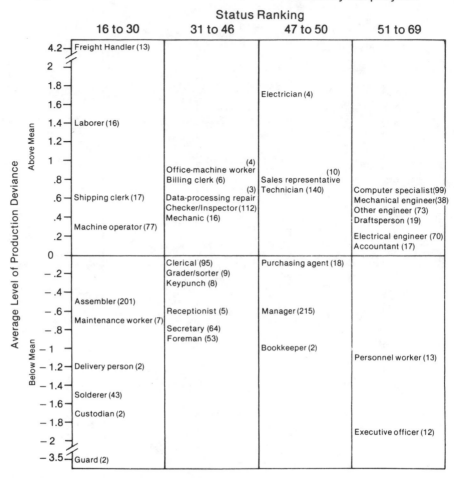

Figure 6-6. Average Level of Production Deviance for Each Occupational Classification, Manufacturing Sector

Unlike retailing, where merchandise and cash have intrinsic economic value, the tools, equipment, and raw materials of an electronics-manufacturing plant have little social or monetary value unless one knows what they can be used for. Our personal employee interviews with manufacturing personnel confirm that electronic components have no direct worth to an assembly-line person, but to the electrical engineer building his own ham radio, microwave, television, microcomputer, or gadget, these items have great worth. It is interesting to note that in this industry sector we found the majority of the inventory controls directed toward the very employees (that is, assembly personnel) to whom the property has little value. Engineers, however, have almost uncontrolled access to tools, equipment, and materials in the manufacturing plant because it is argued that to control stringently these employees would constrain their development and inventive creativity. Thus, we find yet another qualification to the opportunity hypothesis—namely, that access without knowledge of the social and economic value does not yield high levels of theft.

Among hospital employees we again find an inconsistency in our opportunity hypothesis. In the health-care industry, like manufacturing, we observed that most of the property theft was reported by a cluster of the high-status employees—most importantly, the registered nursing staff. With one exception (dishwashers), we found most of the high-property-theft occupations to be those directly responsible for the delivery of patient-care services on the ward. Many other employees in the hospital have equal or greater access to the property that can be taken in a hospital but have lower theft levels (namely, food-service personnel). As with manufacturing, we again find knowledge having a direct effect on theft levels. Despite the recent popularization of so-called surgical greens on college campuses, most of the items with social value in a hospital are only appreciated by the professionals who use them on a daily basis.

Another interesting finding emerges from the hospital employees' responses, providing yet a further refinement to our opportunity theory. Recall that in both retail and manufacturing, essentially the same occupational groups were involved in both property and production deviance. However, in hospitals we found that the nursing/patient-care staff, although more highly involved in property deviance, indicated below-average levels of production or time deviance. The reason for this specialization of deviance may be due to the professional commitment of these patient-care personnel; in committing production deviance the victim would be the patient, not the organization. This observation came through quite clearly in our face-to-face hospital-employee interviews—namely, it is much more acceptable to victimize the hospital organization than to reduce productivity that may have a deleterious effect on the welfare (even lives) of patients. Even if property deviance occurs on the wards, many nurses told us that seldom are items taken that would jeopardize the health or safety of a patient. Thus, for the highly skilled and professionalized hospital employee, higher commitment to patient care than to the hospital organization means that most employee deviance will be directed toward nonessential property of the institution.

In summary, undoubtedly opportunity is an important factor in understanding employee theft and deviance. However, as we have seen, opportunity may be only a secondary factor that constrains the manner in which the deviance will be manifested.

Notes

1. Richard A. Cloward and Lloyd E. Ohlin, *Delinquency and Opportunity: A Theory of Delinquent Gangs* (New York: Free Press, 1960).

2. C.F. Hemphill, Jr., "Cutting Pilferage, Petty Cash Losses," *Administrative Management* 30 (February 1969):40, 42, 44.

7 Job Dissatisfaction and Employee Deviance

Although not often explicitly stated, a single underlying assumption runs through the vast majority of the qualitative field studies of employee deviance—namely, both property and production deviance can be interpreted as a response to the perceived quality of the employment experience. Existing work on the behavioral effects of worker dissatisfaction has concentrated heavily on physical withdrawal from the work place as the dependent variable—for example, turnover,[1] absenteeism,[2] and attendance.[3] Although the available empirical research has been less than completely consistent in its findings, a recent writer concludes that attitudes toward the job can predict work-place behavior but only when such behavior is under the voluntary control of the employee.[4] Thus, in the absence of organizational coercion or constraint, perceptions about the quality of the work experience have been shown to influence employee acts against the organization. However, since the preponderance of available studies concentrates on quitting or not showing up for work, few of the possible while-on-the-job manifestations of deviance have been examined in terms of their relationship to the subjective quality of the employment experience.

The only available empirical study that assesses the association between the perceived level of job satisfaction and both property and production deviance is reported by Mangione and Quinn.[5] Their study is based upon data collected from a separate mini-questionnaire administered to selected respondents from the University of Michigan Survey Research Center's larger 1972-1973 *Quality of Employment Survey.*[6] The authors cautiously conclude that general satisfaction with one's job was related significantly (in the predicted negative direction) to six types of counterproductive and theft behavior, but only for men 30 years of age and older.[7]

Although Mangione and Quinn's study is an innovative and significant piece of research, the data were limited due primarily to the brevity of the one-page instrument included as a self-administered addendum to the *Quality of Employment Survey.*[8] Since job satisfaction was measured by a single general item, it was not possible to identify the relative salience of various perceived dimensions or facets of the work experience.

This chapter builds and expands upon Mangione and Quinn's exploratory work and examines the relationship between both general and specific dimensions of perceived job satisfaction and two separate manifestations of unauthorized worker behavior—namely, property and production deviance.

Measurement

The individual employee's perception of the quality of the work experience was operationalized via three different job-satisfaction measures—specifically, two separate single-item measures in addition to a multidimension index. First, a question that was intended to tap employees' general perception of job satisfaction was presented to the respondent: All in all, how satisfied are you with your present job? (4, very satisfied; 3, somewhat satisfied; 2, somewhat dissatisfied; 1, very dissatisfied). Second, the respondent was asked: Considering how you feel at this time about your job, how likely is it that you will make a genuine effort to find a new job in the next year? (3, very likely; 2, somewhat likely; 1, not at all likely). Finally, a series of shorter items intended to measure various distinct dimensions of job satisfaction was presented to the respondent. Fifty statements, in large part drawn from the 1977 University of Michigan survey,[9] were presented to respondents whom we then asked to indicate whether the statement was very true (4), somewhat true (3), not very true (2), or not at all true (1) about their particular jobs.

Using both varimax-factor and reliability-analysis techniques, eight distinct dimensions of job statisfaction were derived, each reflecting a unique aspect of the work experience. These job-satisfaction dimensions consist primarily of slightly regrouped University of Michigan items, plus an additional dimension constructed from original items. The eight job-satisfaction dimensions, including the thirty specific items, are presented in table 7-1 along with the item-to-total correlations and Cronbach's Alphas.

Each of the eight job-satisfaction dimensions addresses a distinct aspect of the work experience. The first focuses on the employee's appraisal of the fairness and ethical standards exhibited by his or her employer. The nature of the relationships with co-workers is the second dimension. The third dimension concerns the employee's evaluation of his or her immediate supervisor's performance. Whether or not the employee has been given enough information and authority to get the job done is our fourth dimension. The extent to which the job provides adequate task challenges is the underlying factor of the fifth dimension. The sixth dimension concerns the quantity of the daily work load required of each employee. Finally, the seventh and eighth dimensions refer to perceived satisfaction with pay and promotional opportunities. A separate score was derived for these eight dimensions by summing the item responses to each.

General Job Satisfaction and Employee Deviance

When we compared our general measure of job satisfaction to self-reported involvement in both property theft and production deviance, as expected,

Table 7-1
Dimensions of Perceived Job Satisfaction

Dimensions	Item-to-Total Correlation
Factor 1: Employer (Cronbach's Alpha = .80)	
My employer cares about his/her employees.	.66
My employer seeks to provide safe working conditions.	.51
My employer is honest.	.64
My employer is fair in handling of complaints by employees.	.66
Factor 2: Co-workers (Cronbach's Alpha = .65)	
The people I work with take a personal interest in me. [M]	.48
The people I work with are friendly. [M]	.49
I have a lot in common with the people I work with.	.44
Factor 3: Supervisor (Cronbach's Alpha = .88)	
My supervisor is successful at getting people to work together. [M]	.70
My supervisor is friendly. [M]	.69
My supervisor is helpful to me in getting my job done.	.74
My supervisor is competent in doing his/her job. [M]	.71
My supervisor is very concerned about the welfare of those under him/her. [M]	.74
Factor 4: Information and Authority (Cronbach's Alpha = .71)	
I have enough information to get the job done. [M]	.48
I feel like I know what's going on at work.	.44
My responsibilities are clearly defined [M]	.57
I have enough authority to do my job. [M]	.50
Factor 5: Task Challenges (Cronbach's Alpha = .79)	
I have an opportunity to develop my own special abilities. [M]	.63
The work is interesting. [M]	.55
I am given a lot of freedom to decide how I do my own work. [M]	.53
I am given a chance to do the things I do best. [M]	.69
I can see the results of my work. [M]	.46
Factor 6: Work Load (Cronbach's Alpha = .73)	
I receive enough help and equipment to get the job done. [M]	.53
I am not asked to do excessive amounts of work. [M]	.58
I am free from the conflicting demands that other people make of me. [M]	.43
I have enough time to get the job done. [M]	.56
Factor 7: Pay (Cronbach's Alpha = .65)	
The pay is good. [M]	.49
My fringe benefits are good. [M]	.49
Factor 8: Promotional Opportunity (Cronbach's Alpha = .77)	
The chances for promotion are good. [M]	.54
Promotions are handled fairly. [M]	.61
My employer is concerned about giving everyone a chance to get ahead. [M]	.66

[M] = Item used in University of Michigan Survey Research Center's *1972-73 Quality of Employment Survey* (Ann Arbor: University of Michigan, 1974).

we found negative associations. Although weakest in the manufacturing sample ($r = -.06$), table 7-2 presents correlations of $-.09$ and $-.11$ between job satisfaction and property deviance among retail and hospital employees, respectively. For production deviance we can report even stronger zero-order correlation coefficients, ranging from $-.19$ in the hospital sector to $-.23$ in the retail sector. We may conclude that those employees who were generally more dissatisfied with the quality of their employment experience were also likely to be more involved in deviant acts against the work place—both taking property and engaging in counterproductive behavior. The second of our quality-of-work-experience measures, the employee's estimate of the likelihood of leaving the job, was found, as hypothesized, to be related positively to both property and production deviance. Specifically, when we examined the relationship between an employee's intention to leave the job in the near future and property deviance, we found correlations among retail and hospital employees of .18 and .11 respectively, with a positive (but somewhat weaker) association for manufacturing employees. Additionally, we observed that the employee's assessment of future continuation with one's present job was even more strongly associated with production deviance in all three industry sectors. Thus, these data suggest that those employees who did not expect to continue working for their present employers exhibited a greater propensity for work-place theft and counterproductive behavior.

Specific Job Satisfaction and Employee Deviance

Since our general measure of job satisfaction was found to be correlated negatively to both property and production deviance, we expected that many of the eight specific dimensions of job satisfaction would also predict deviance involvement. An examination of the lower half of table 7-2 confirms that this is indeed the case. With the exception of property deviance in manufacturing, most job-satisfaction dimensions indicate significant negative correlations with both property and production deviance.

When we specifically examined property deviance and our eight dimensions of job satisfaction for the retail and hospital employees, all relationships (except co-worker satisfaction, which is theoretically independent from the other factors) were found to be significant ($p \leq .05$) and in the predicted negative direction. Among manufacturing respondents we found only dissatisfaction with two dimensions, employer and authority, to be associated with our property-deviance dependent variable at the $p \leq .05$ level of significance.

While our various measures of job satisfaction correlated reasonably well with property-deviance involvement for retail and hospital employees,

Table 7-2
Pearson Product-Moment Correlations with Property and Production Deviance, by Industry Sector

Independent Variables	Property Deviance			Production Deviance		
	Retail	Manufacturing	Hospital	Retail	Manufacturing	Hospital
General satisfaction	−.11 (−.07)	−.06 (*)	−.09 (−.06)	−.23 (−.17)	−.20 (−.17)	−.19 (−.15)
Looking for a job	.18 (.08)	.06 (*)	.11 (.06)	.30 (.14)	.19 (.12)	.20 (.12)
Dimensions						
1. Employer	−.12 (−.10)	−.05 (*)	−.11 (−.09)	−.22 (−.16)	−.17 (−.16)	−.18 (−.14)
2. Co-workers	−.04 (*)	* (*)	* (*)	−.07 (−.04)	−.07 (−.07)	−.04 (−.03)
3. Supervisor	−.09 (−.06)	* (*)	−.08 (−.06)	−.18 (−.15)	−.11 (−.11)	−.17 (−.15)
4. Information and authority	−.06 (*)	−.09 (−.09)	−.08 (−.06)	−.13 (−.08)	−.15 (−.14)	−.12 (−.09)
5. Task challenges	−.13 (−.06)	* (*)	−.05 (*)	−.23 (−.13)	−.18 (−.17)	−.15 (−.11)
6. Work load	−.06 (−.04)	* (*)	−.06 (−.04)	−.12 (−.10)	−.07 (−.07)	−.06 (−.03)
7. Pay	−.09 (−.06)	* (*)	−.06 (−.03)	−.13 (−.10)	−.13 (−.10)	−.06 (*)
8. Promotional opportunity	−.09 (−.09)	* (*)	−.06 (−.05)	−.15 (−.16)	−.16 (−.18)	−.16 (−.15)
Age	−.26	−.17	−.18	−.40	−.31	−.28

Note: Partials controlling for age are in parentheses.
*Not statistically significant at the .05 level.

relationships for the manufacturing sample consistently were weak or non-existent. The lack of a significant relationship possibly is attributable to the reduced social worth of the property that can be taken in an electronics-manufacturing plant. Instead, in this situation of limited intrinsic property worth, we would expect that employee dissatisfaction would manifest itself behaviorally in deviance against the norms of production, not property. This explanation seems to be confirmed by the data.

When we examined our second dependent variable, production deviance, table 7-2 indicates much greater consistency among the three industry sectors in that all eight job-satisfaction dimensions were significant at the $p \leq .05$ level. The relative strengths of manufacturing coefficients for production deviance were equal to, or in some cases exceeded, those found in retail and hospitals, suggesting that dissatisfaction among manufacturing employees was much more likely to manifest itself in violation of production norms rather than property theft.

Since recent research continues to suggest a significant positive relationship between employee age and satisfaction with employment, age was included as a control variable in the analysis.[10] Our data are, in fact, consistent with this finding, with zero-order correlations ranging from .12 to .20 between age and our general satisfaction variable. This relationship, in addition to the fact that we observed significant negative correlations between age and employee deviance (shown in table 7-2 as ranging from $-.17$ to $-.40$), prompted us to inquire whether our negative coefficients between job satisfaction and deviance might simply be a function of the employee's age—that is, does the younger worker's relatively greater dissatisfaction with the employment experience and correspondingly higher incidence of deviance yield a spurious relationship between these two variables, especially in the retail and hospital industries that have greater concentrations of younger employees?

When age was held constant most relationships between job satisfaction and employee deviance remained significant, although slightly reduced in magnitude. For example, partials (contained in parentheses) from table 7-2 indicate coefficients between property theft and our general satisfaction variable were reduced approximately by one-third. Controlling for age reduced our measure of the likelihood-of-leaving-the-job association with property theft by approximately one-half in the retail and hospital samples, disappearing entirely for manufacturing.

When we examined our specific dimensions of job satisfaction, we found that controlling for age negated relatively few previously significant correlations. For example, in retail only dissatisfaction with co-workers and information and authority seemed to be a function of age. In manufacturing, one of our two significant dimensions was explained by the age of the employee—dissatisfaction with employer. In hospitals, opportunities for challenging tasks seemed to be explained by age inasmuch as age often is covariant with tenure, seniority, and occupational status. Thus, while the variable age did neutralize some of our previously observed relationships (especially in retail), we certainly have not discovered a spurious correlation between property theft and job satisfaction.

These results follow similar patterns when production deviance was correlated with our quality-of-work measures while controlling for the age of the employee. Most relationships were only slightly reduced in magnitude, while the remainder correlated at the same level with even an occasional increase in strength. In only one instance, pay satisfaction in hospitals, did age account for the previously observed relationship. Thus, even though many younger workers perceived a greater level of dissatisfaction with the employment experience, this factor alone did not explain the preponderance of negative relationships found between job satisfaction and deviant behavior by employees against the work organization.

Conclusion

Dissatisfaction with the quality of the work experience has long been recognized as an important factor in predicting a diverse range of occupationally related behaviors. Consistent with that tradition, these data have attempted to link worker dissatisfaction with two theoretically related categories of on-the-job employee deviance—namely, property and production deviance. Among samples of retail and hospital employees, we were able to demonstrate negative correlations between work-place attitudes and theft of money and property from the company. Additionally, in each of the three industry sectors surveyed, we established an empirical relationship between job dissatisfaction and a number of counterproductive employee activities such as slow or sloppy workmanship, sick-leave abuse, and tardiness.

Recognizing the disproportionately greater levels of job dissatisfaction and employee deviance among contemporary younger workers, age was explored as a potential antecedent factor (see also chapter 5). When the age of the employee was controlled, however, it became clear that this variable accounted for a relatively minor proportion of the explained variance. In short, these findings suggest that all age groups of employees who are dissatisfied with the quality of their present employment experience, especially the younger worker, are significantly more likely to seek unauthorized redress for these perceived inequities from the organization via its tangible property or expected levels of productivity.

Given the minimal strength of the relationships reported here, we cannot claim to have explained employee deviance. Job dissatisfaction is apparently only one variable set related to the occurrence of deviance within the work setting. However, when we compare these quantitative results to the rich literature of qualitative field studies, the observed consistency in the findings allows us to conclude that employee deviance is best understood within the social context of the work environment that includes perceived job dissatisfaction as a principal component. For example, Jason Ditton documents a lengthy history of "wages-in-kind" through which employees "situated in structurally disadvantaged parts [of the organization] receive large segments of their wages invisibly."[11] The anthropologist Gerald Mars has observed consistently that in both the hotel dining room and among maritime dock workers, pilferage was not viewed as theft,[12] but instead it was "seen as a morally justified addition to wages; indeed, as an entitlement due from exploiting employers."[13] Other sources of field data on the phenomenon of employee deviance reported by David Altheide et al. indicated that theft is often perceived by employees as a "way of getting back at the boss or supervisor."[14] The Altheide study informants, like the survey respondents in this book, indicated that job satisfaction was even more important than wages in affecting the "social meaning of employee theft."[15] In summary, the available data, both qualitative and quantitative, strongly support the theoretical model that views deviance by employees as a reaction to the social conditions internal, not external, to the work milieu.

Theodore Kemper argues that this social-context model of employee theft and counterproductive behavior theoretically is more consistent with traditional sociological explanations of deviance that are based upon structural variables present in the formal work organization.[16] Kemper predicts that "when the organization as an entity, or in the person of a superior, has defaulted on the obligations of the organization to its members, reciprocal deviance can result."[17] By reciprocal deviance Kemper refers to employee behavior that is punitive in nature, intended to reconcile organizational failures to "recognize merit" (for example, dissatisfaction with pay and promotional opportunity), or an "inordinate increase in amount of work expected" (for example, dissatisfaction with work load, task challenges, and information and authority).[18] Further, if the upper levels of the organization exhibit behavior that could be interpreted as deviant or unethical by lower levels of employees, Kemper expects to find instances of "parallel deviance" where employees mirror the questionable example set by their superiors (for example, dissatisfaction with employer and supervisor).[19]

The reader is reminded that this book has concentrated on a limited aspect of the total work experience: the subjective perceptions of individual employees. Undoubtedly, more research will be necessary before we comprehend adequately the other complex sets of variables that affect deviance in the work place.[20] The major thrust of this book suggests, however, that the most theoretically salient studies will be those that focus on factors intrinsic to the nature of the present employment experience.

Notes

1. James L. Price, *A Study of Turnover* (Ames: Iowa State University Press, 1977).

2. L.W. Porter and R.M. Steers, "Organizational Work and Personal Factors in Employee Turnover and Absenteeism," *Psychological Bulletin* 80 (1973):151-176.

3. F.J. Smith, "Work Attitudes as Predictors of Attendance on a Specific Day," *Journal of Applied Psychology* 62 (1977):16-19.

4. J.B. Herman, "Are Situational Contingencies Limiting Job Attitude-Job Performance Relationships?" *Organizational Behavior and Human Performance* 10 (1973):208-224.

5. T.W. Mangione and R.P Quinn, "Job Satisfaction, Counter-Productive Behavior, and Drug Use at Work," *Journal of Applied Psychology* 11 (1975):114-116.

6. Robert P. Quinn and Linda Shepard, *The 1972-73 Quality of Employment Survey: Descriptive Statistics with Comparison Data from the 1969-70 Survey of Working Conditions* (Ann Arbor: Institute of Social Research, University of Michigan, 1974).

7. Mangione and Quinn, "Job Satisfaction."

8. Ibid.

9. Robert P. Quinn and Graham L. Staines, *1977 Quality of Employment Survey: Descriptive Statistics with Comparison Data from 1969-70 and 1972-73 Surveys* (Ann Arbor: Institute of Social Research, University of Michigan, 1979).

10. J.D. Wright and R.F. Hamilton, "Work Satisfaction and Age: Some Evidence for the 'Job Change' Hypothesis," *Social Forces* 56 (1978):1140-1158.

11. J. Ditton, "Perks, Pilferage, and the Fiddle: The Historical Structure of Invisible Wages," *Theory and Society* 4 (1977):39-71.

12. G. Mars, "Chance, Punters, and the Fiddle: Institutionalized Pilferage in a Hotel Dining Room," in *The Sociology of the Workplace*, ed. M. Warner (New York: Halsted Press, 1973), pp. 200-210; and Mars, "Dock Pilferage: A Case Study in Occupational Theft," in *Deviance and Social Control*, eds. Paul Rock and Mary McIntosh (London: Tavistock, 1974), pp. 209-228.

13. Ibid., p. 224.

14. D.L. Altheide, et al., "The Social Meanings of Employee Theft," in *Crime at the Top*, eds. John M. Johnson and Jack D. Douglas (Philadelphia: Lippincott, 1978), pp. 90-124.

15. Ibid.

16. T.D. Kemper, "Representative Roles and the Legitimization of Deviance," *Social Problems* 13 (1966):288-298.

17. Ibid., pp. 293-295.

18. Ibid.

19. Ibid.

20. For an earlier discussion of these variables with Phase I data only, see R.C. Hollinger and J.P. Clark, "Employee Deviance: A Response to the Perceived Quality of the Work Experience," *Work and Occupations* 9 (1982):97-114.

8 Formal Organizational Controls and Property Deviance

with *Peter F. Parilla*

Organizations are not usually passive victims of employee deviance. On the contrary, a concerted effort is made within most organizations to control employee behavior and to protect corporate property. This chapter examines formal measures aimed at shaping employee behavior. Our specific goal is to evaluate whether certain organizational-control efforts do, in fact, lead to a reduction in the prevalence of employee theft of company property.

Organizational Control

Organizational theorists have emphasized for many years the importance of control in complex or formal organizations. Indeed, it can be argued that the problem of control is more acute in complex organizations than in any other type of social organization.[1] Unlike the family or the community, formal organizations are created intentionally to achieve certain limited objectives. Because of this goal orientation, organizations are extremely reliant upon deliberate control efforts to shape member behavior in order to meet these objectives. Particularly in a free-market environment, effectively concentrating organizational efforts determines to a considerable extent the competitive position of the company.

One employee activity that clearly interferes with effective goal attainment is employee theft. Such theft hampers organizational productivity and profitability in at least two ways. First, stolen property must be replaced. Consequently, resources of time and money are diverted from the direct pursuit of organizational goals. Second, the loss of materials from theft may lead to disruptions or uncertainties within an organization. Organizations cannot function smoothly if essential materials are unavailable when they are needed. In short, organizations have a vested interest in controlling employee theft. In this discussion, we focus on several relatively common control mechanisms intended to accomplish this task, including company policy, selection of personnel, inventory control, security, and punishment.

Peter F. Parilla is the principal author of this chapter.

Control through Policy

In the bureaucratic model of organizations, formalized policies and rules are considered fundamental methods for maintaining control. Workers are told explicitly what they are expected to do and are held accountable for its being accomplished.[2] Prior research has demonstrated that organizational policies in fact affect employee behavior. For example, in the case of absenteeism, the existence of a strict policy has been related to a decrease in this activity.[3] Therefore, one might expect similar results for policies governing employee theft.

The treatment of employee theft as a matter for policy may serve a variety of functions in an organization. The most obvious of these is one of clarification and deterrence. A corporate policy could serve as a formal announcement that the taking of organizational property is considered to be a serious matter and will be treated as such. Thus, employees may refrain from stealing because they honor the organization's procedures on behavior toward its property and fear the consequences if found in violation of this policy.

An important related argument is that the presence of policy increases the likelihood that supervisors will react when theft is discovered. The fact that a supervisor is backed by corporate policy may help him or her overcome the hesitancy often associated with reacting to such a sensitive matter. As Gouldner argues, one function of bureaucratic rules is that rule enforcement becomes viewed as a job requirement, not as a personal option or vendetta.[4] In addition, rules tend to legitimate the use of management sanctions because they constitute a public warning as to the type of behavior that will provoke sanctioning. A rule creates a climate of fairness because the person acted against has been forewarned that his action could result in punishment. In short, supervisors feel they are in a securer legal and ethical position to take action in a theft case if a specific policy backs them up.

Threatening punishment and guiding supervisors, however, are not the sole functions that antitheft policy may serve. Through the promulgation and communication of policy, management may try to create a normative climate in which people prefer not to steal. For example, it is likely that most employees want to consider themselves, and have others view them, as being honest. Still, these same employees often can take home certain types of corporate goods without thinking about it. The reason for this apparent inconsistency is that neither employees nor their co-workers define the taking of this property as stealing.[5] The role corporate policy plays in this regard may be to convince employees that taking from the company is no different than stealing from another individual—something most employees would never consider. A concerted policy effort may seek to accentuate the fact that the taking of organizational property is not a perk—it is theft.

In a similar vein, policy may be focused on educating employees about employee theft. Many employees view theft in terms of discrete acts that, viewed separately, cost an organization little. What employees often fail to consider is the aggregated consequences of such activity. If employees were to appreciate the cumulative effects and how those effects must be passed on to customers or patients, they might willingly cease their own theft behavior and even attempt to convince other employees to do the same. In sum, if organizational policy can be used to persuade employees that the taking of corporate property has both moral and financial implications, theft may be reduced greatly. Moreover, this reduction may be attained not through heavy-handed threats but through the establishment of a normative system in which workers themselves discourage theft. In conclusion, we would hypothesize that organizations that develop and disseminate an antitheft policy will suffer less employee theft.

Control through Hiring

An important but commonly ignored aspect of organizational control is the ability of the organization to select its members.[6] Control is exerted through the hiring of persons who best will conform to organizational expectations and the exclusion of applicants who will not. Thus, the task of corporate gatekeepers is to identify and hire employees who are least likely to violate organizational norms. In conducting evaluations of potential employees, however, the primary focus typically is upon whether they possess requisite job skills, not upon their honesty. Corporate officials also realize that it is counterproductive to hire an individual who is technically competent but who would directly or indirectly deplete an organization's resources by engaging in theft or other disruptive behavior. Therefore, an organization would benefit by identifying such individuals and denying them membership.

The idea that it is desirable and possible to identify and screen out dishonest persons follows from the so-called bad-apple theory of employee theft. This theory assumes that within a population of potential employees, some individuals will have a propensity toward theft. If they become employees, these bad apples will steal from the organization, and the presence of these individuals in the organization may somehow influence law-abiding employees to violate antitheft norms. The bad-apple theory has gained considerable currency in security and personnel circles, yet there is a paucity of empirical support for it.

Typically, a variety of pre-employment-screening methods are utilized to judge an applicant's honesty. Potential sources of information are impressions given by a candidate himself, recommendations from former employers or other references, and more-impersonal quantitative assessments such as polygraph examinations and personality tests. Using some combination of these sources, the person doing the hiring tries to assess whether the applicant is a potential troublemaker. Certainly, the ability to select is less than perfect. A major reason for this selection problem is that the mechanisms used for screening on honesty are quite fallible. They possess a number of inherent limitations and constraints that revolve around the sheer difficulty of gathering information about an issue as sensitive as previous employee-theft involvement. Despite its limitations, background checks and hiring interviews do at times uncover information that allows for more-rational selection to take place. One would be hard put to argue the opposite case that ignorance is superior to some, albeit partial, data on applicants.

Moreover, rigorous screening may provide an additional benefit in terms of the reduction of employee theft. If an organization obtains a reputation for thorough pre-employment checking, a person who has a history of known thefts may be dissuaded from applying. The consequence is that one less potential thief is included in the pool of job candidates. In conclusion, based upon this discussion, one would expect that organizations with more-intensive pre-employment screening will have less employee theft.

Control through Inventory Control

A third approach to the control of employee theft is related to inventory control, even though the systems to be discussed here are not devised primarily to prevent theft. Most are considered standard accounting and inventory practices that are instituted to assure that organizational assets are used in a cost-effective manner. Thus, even if employee theft were not a concern, these practices would be required to provide accurate information about the quantities and deployment of various corporate assets.

An additional benefit of thorough accounting and inventory controls, however, relates to the prevalence of employee theft. The same procedures that an organization intitiates to detect errors, avoid waste, and ensure accurate record keeping also can serve as a protection against employee theft. Inventory records, which are necessary to maintain adequate supplies, also can signal that materials are being stolen.

There are several ways in which inventory controls should affect a company's theft rate. First, an organization that closely monitors its assets would possess more-reliable and up-to-date information about the occurrence and amount of suspicious property disappearances. Gathering such information is a necessary first step in taking effective action against the problem. Second, since many controls are designed to prohibit certain employees from gaining access to protected assets, a company using such controls could more easily trace losses to those employees who are authorized to handle these assets. If employees know that they can be held accountable for these losses, they are more likely to be deterred from thieving. Finally, efforts directed at the operation of a materials-management system may be interpreted by the work force as a sign of management's concern for asset protection. If this concern is perceived to be high, employees may be more reluctant to engage in larcenous behaviors. With this rationale in mind, we hypothesized that those organizations judged to have the more-sophisticated inventory-control systems would have less employee theft.

Control through Security

Of all the organizational controls that might be directed at employee theft, those implemented by security departments are perhaps the most obvious and direct. Security, more than any other department in an organization, is given primary responsibility for controlling the problem of internal theft. To achieve this goal, security officers are engaged in numerous proactive and reactive measures (for example, making rounds, surveillance, and theft investigations) that aim to counteract theft behavior. Through these activities, they seek to instill in employees the perception that employee theft will result in apprehension and punishment. Because of this deterrent effect, we would hypothesize that the greater the security effort of an organization, the lower would be that firm's internal theft problem.

Control through Punishment

A final means through which organizational officials can control employee theft is by sanctioning apprehended offenders. Theoretically, punishing those who have stolen should deter others in the work force from engaging in theft in the future. For internal theft, a number of sanctioning options are available. These include one or more of the following: doing nothing after apprehension, internal discipline but with retention of the employee, termination of the worker, restitution, and/or criminal prosecution.

Previous research on the deterrent effects of punishment demonstrates that the greatest deterrent effect is derived by making punishment relatively certain.[7] We would expect these same relationships to hold for employee theft and predict that the greater the certainty of punishment, the lower the incidence of theft.

Prior research on deterrence is less clear as to whether an increase in severity of punishment has a similar effect.[8] It may well be that for a crime like employee theft, the harshness of the sanction is of minor consequence.[9] A mild sanction may have the same deterrent effect as a harsher one. Thus, we would hypothesize that severity of punishment is not a significant factor in deterring employee theft.

Methods: Measures of Organizational Controls

The independent variables to be studied in this chapter rely primarily on materials gathered in the executive interviews and searches of corporate records (see chapter 2). The following sections provide the operational definitions of these variables.

Policy

The first index was developed to determine whether organizational policy addresses the issue of employee theft and, if so, the degree to which management communicates that policy to employees. In order to rank organizations on their policy stance toward employee dishonesty, we asked corporate executives to provide the following information:

Did the organization possess a formal written policy or rules prohibiting employee dishonesty?

Were new employees made aware of this policy either verbally or in writing during their new-employee orientation?

Was the policy disseminated to all employees or just certain occupational groups?

Was the topic of employee theft covered in any other forum other than orientation, such as newsletters and bulletin boards?

Each organization's index score resulted from the summation of the scores on these four items. (Cronbach's Alpha for the policy index constructed from the items was .782).

Pre-Employment Screening

To determine the degree to which an organization controlled theft through selection, we asked personnel directors to describe the extent of pre-employment screening performed by their departments. Specifically, we sought to know whether a candidate's application was accepted at face value or whether inquiries were made into the person's background. Data were gathered regarding five specific areas where follow-up investigations could be made: (1) references, (2) job history, (3) conviction record, (4) extent of indebtedness, and (5) previous involvement in employee theft. (Some of this information such as conviction records and past involvement in employee theft is not readily available. Some organizations do attempt to obtain this material, however, through informal networks with either the police or acquaintances in other organizations.) Each item was coded 4 to 1 depending on whether information was investigated for all candidates, most candidates, some, or none. Based on the results of a factor analysis, two separate dimensions seem to underlie these five items.

Two of the items—checking on references and job history—are geared toward measuring previous occupational performance. Thus, we combined the two to form an index that we called performance checks. (The Cronbach's Alpha for this index was .848.)

The remaining three items bear more directly on obtaining information on problem areas in a person's past. The index created by adding together the items of conviction record, indebtedness, and prior involvement in theft was called problem checks. (This index had a Cronbach's Alpha of .750.)

Inventory Controls

Of the control systems we attempted to measure, inventory control posed the most serious problems. Limitations of time and money prohibited us from trying to conduct operational audits or tests of the internal-control systems of each of the forty-seven organizations. Even if these had been possible, it would have been difficult for us validly to compare and rank the quality of such highly complex and diverse systems. Consequently, our measures of inventory control rely upon executives' personal evaluations of these systems. Specifically, we asked those executives most knowledgeable of their organization's controls (for example, inventory-control officers, materials-management directors, and internal auditors) to assess the impact of their control systems upon employee theft.

Clearly, these measures are less objective than our other indicators of control. In addition, there is the danger that officials whom we interviewed would feel a responsibility to defend their systems and thus to provide invalid data. In defense of these measures, however, two comments might be made. First, many inventory-control specialists did not view theft control as a high priority of their systems. Thus, they had little invested in their evaluations concerning their system's effect on theft. Second, a sufficient number of officers gave negative evaluations of their systems to suggest that they were not overestimating the capabilities of these controls.

To measure the ability of inventory controls to curtail theft, we asked executives to provide their opinions on the following topics:

To what extent was theft control viewed as a high or low priority within the control systems?

How satisfied were they with inventory controls as those controls related to the control of employee theft?

How vulnerable was the firm's inventory to theft by employees?

Security

In our examination of security departments, we sought to measure certain structural characteristics associated with them. Three relevant dimensions were tapped.

The first index, called security sophistication, examined the degree to which an organization's security department was a specialized function directed by experts in the field. In order to measure this dimension, we obtained the following information:

Does the organization have a functionary identified as a security director? If so, does this individual perform the task on a full-time or part-time basis?

Is the security director a security professional? Does he have previous law-enforcement experience, and does he participate in the larger security community by belonging to a professional security association (for example, the American Society for Industrial Security)?

What is the nature of the security staff? Is there a full-time, in-house staff, or are security personnel hired from outside agencies like contract guards?

(The Cronbach's Alpha for the security-sophistication index constructed from these items was .879.)

The second security indicator, security size, measured the number of full-time equivalents on the security-department staff. In order to be sure that this was not just a reflection of total organizational size, we computed a ratio consisting of the number of the number of security staff divided by the number of total employees.

Finally, for the third index, security priority, we sought to measure how the prevention and detection of employee theft compared to other security responsibilities. In order to assess security priority, we asked security directors to examine a list of sixteen duties often assigned to security departments. Three of these tasks dealt with forms of employee theft. We then asked the directors to select the duties for which their department had responsibility. Of those chosen, we requested that the directors rate the five most important duties and the five on which the department spent the most time. Our scale on security priority is a composite based on the number of times the director claimed that the three employee-theft items were part of the department's responsibility, one of the five most important duties, and one of the top five to which time was devoted. (Cronbach's Alpha for the security-priority index was .757.)

Punishment

In order to assess the impact of punishment on employee theft, we collected data regarding the apprehension and disposition of employee offenders. Because security records were often kept at an aggregate level, the measures of punishment are relatively crude. For instance, it is not possible to determine which particular combinations of punishment have the highest deterrent value. The data we were able to gather involved:

Apprehensions: Number of employees apprehended for theft in the previous year;

Terminations: Percentage of apprehended employees who were terminated by the organization;

Prosecutions: Percentage of apprehended employees who were referred for prosecution;

Restitution: Percentage of apprehended employees who made some restitution for their theft.

Statistical Analysis

Before reporting the findings, we must comment briefly on the statistical procedures that we utilized. In the forthcoming analysis we used two different measures of association. When independent variables are at an interval level, we utilize a Pearson's product-moment correlation. When independent variables are ordinal, relationships are measured with Kendall's rank-order correlation Tau b. In this analysis, Kendall's Tau b was chosen over gammas, which are shown in other parts of the book, for two reasons. First, it is the most suitable ordinal measure to use if two or more cases receive the same score for a variable (that is, tied cases), and second, Tau b is an appropriate statistic for relatively small samples. Since this part of the analysis is based on subsamples of twenty-one, sixteen, and ten organizations, rather than thousands of individuals, this was an important criterion for the analysis.

Another comment that should be made at this point relates to the use of significance tests in our analysis. The sample of organziations studied was selected nonrandomly. Thus, the use of significance tests is problematic. One the one hand, the lack of a random sample creates difficulties with regard to inferences. Without a random sample, selection biases and problems of nonrepresentativeness are much more likely. With such a situation, providing significance levels can be misleading to the reader. On the other hand, failure to include tests of significance deprives the reader of one more bit of information with which to judge the merit of the reported relationships. The significance level furnishes a form of a yardstick by which one can estimate the likelihood that relationships are real as opposed to chance occurrences. Thus, we were faced with a dilemma as to whether or not levels of statistical significance should be included in the organizational analysis. The decision was made to provide them, thinking that they furnished additional data for the reader. When in doubt, we felt it would be better to err in favor of reporting facts that might be useful in interpreting the data. Thus, in the organizational analysis one should be most cautious in interpreting significance levels.

Organizational Rates of Property Deviance

In the analysis presented in this chapter, we try to shed some light on the issue of organizational-theft rates. First, we examine the variation in rates of employee theft and levels of organizational control from organization to organization. Second, we explore how theft rates are related to various forms of organizational control.

Before proceeding, however, two caveats are in order. First, it is important for the reader to realize that in this part of our analysis the organization, not the individual, is our unit of analysis. Instead of studying subsamples of 3,567 retail workers, 4,111 hospital employees, and 1,497 manufacturing workers, this chapter examines sixteen retail store corporations, twenty-one hospitals, and ten electronics-manufacturing firms. Second, one must be very careful in terms of the conclusions drawn from this analysis. The relationships with which we are dealing are between organizational-level variables. To conclude additionally that these relationships also hold true for each of the individual members of these organizations is not justified. In making such an inference comes a danger of committing what social scientists call an ecological fallacy. One cannot assume that relationships describing organizations hold true for all individuals within them.[10]

The first question to be addressed in our analysis examines whether rates of employee theft do, in fact, differ from organization to organization. One method of determining this is to compare the percentage of each firm's work force that is involved in theft. Table 8-1 provides the average percentage of involvement for each industry sector. In addition, standard deviations and ranges are presented to illustrate the degree of differences across organizations. As table 8-1 shows, the percentage of individuals involved in theft does vary within each industry. For retail firms, the percentage of persons involved in employee theft ranged from 19.2 percent at one end of the continuum to 76.9 percent at the other. In the hospitals with the least theft, only 17.7 percent of employees admitted stealing, whereas the figure was 41.7 percent in the hospital with the most individuals involved. Finally, manufacturing firms demonstrate slightly less variations, with a range from 20 percent to 37.8 percent.

It is important to realize what these data do and do not tell us. First, in all organizations, some theft was reported. At least 15 percent of the respondents from each organization admitted to some theft behavior. If nothing else, this tells us that no matter what the organizations had done to prevent theft, some employees were still able to beat the system. Second, in no organization did all employees report stealing. Even in organizations where conditions were such that many employees were engaged in theft, a large proportion remained honest. Finally, it should be noted that in most organizations, involvement in theft was confined to less than half the workers. In only six organizations did a majority of workers admit to taking property.

We once again remind the reader that direct comparisons among the three industry sectors are problematic. Thus, one should not conclude that

Table 8-1
Descriptive Statistics: Percentage Involvement in Employee Theft per Organization, by Sector

Sector	Mean	Standard Deviation	Range
Retail	41.8	18.3	19.2 to 76.9
Hospital	32.2	6.4	17.7 to 41.7
Manufacturing	26.2	5.9	20 to 37.8

more theft exists in one industry than in another. In addition, while the data provide some feeling for the number of people involved in theft, they tell us little about how much or how often employees steal. A more-sensitive measure of theft in organizations is the organizational-theft rate described in chapter 3. This rate, based on the mean of the self-reported theft involvement of individuals in each organization, provides a better indicator of how rampant theft is because it is based on the frequency of occurrence and not just on the number of employees involved.

Table 8-2 contains some descriptive data concerning these organizational-theft rates. Unfortunately, because of the need to standardize scores to reflect seriousness of offense (see chapter 3), the rate that we have obtained does not lend itself to an easy or intuitive interpretation. Two bits of information may aid the reader in interpreting the meaning of these rates. First, if an individual reported no theft involvement, his or her score would be -1.55 in retail, -1.33 in hospitals, and -1.49 in manufacturing. Thus, if there had been an organization in which no theft occurred, the rate of theft would be -1.55 for retail, -1.33 for hospitals, and -1.49 for manufacturing. Second, if the rate of theft for an organization were identical to the mean theft score for its sector, the rate for that organization would be zero. This holds true for each of the three industry sectors. We utilize this organizational-theft rate in the upcoming analysis.

Descriptive Data on Organizational Controls

In addition to explaining variation on the dependent variable, we also examined the degree to which organizations differ in terms of antitheft controls. In table 8-3 we find several descriptive statistics that provide some insight into the extent of control across the three sectors. Looking first at policy, we see that retail firms tended to stress antitheft policy slightly more than hospitals. The manufacturing companies in our sample were a distant third and thus seemed to place little policy emphasis on employee theft.

The two pre-employment-screening indexes show a somewhat different pattern. Hospitals did a slightly more-thorough job of screening on prior

Table 8-2
Descriptive Statistics: Organizational-Theft Rates, by Sector

Sector	Mean	Standard Deviation	Range
Retail	.417	1.1	$-.899$ to 3.17
Hospital	$-.012$	.399	$-.770$ to $.934$
Manufacturing	$-.143$	.379	$-.690$ to $.470$

Table 8-3
Descriptive Statistics: Organizational Controls, by Sector

	Retail		Hospital		Manufacturing	
Control	Mean	Standard Deviation	Mean	Standard Deviation	Mean	Standard Deviation
Policy	5	2.42	3.71	2	1.4	1.89
Screening						
Performance	6.3	1.77	6.86	.459	6.4	1.57
Problems	6.3	2.18	3.71	.230	4.1	.88
Inventory						
Priority	2.8	1.50	2.76	.99	2.65	1.39
Vulnerability	1.5	.60	2.	.55	2.30	.55
Satisfaction	3	.50	2.7	.35	2.80	.58
Security						
Size	35.7	32	14.3	11.4	15.7	25
Sophistication	4.9	2.25	3.95	1.96	2.3	2.16
Priority	7.2	3.08	6.2	1.99	5.1	3.41

job performance than either retail or manufacturing companies. This might be due to the need to certify that applicants possess the requisite skills necessary in their work. Checks on problem areas, however, were more detailed in the retail firms than in the other two sectors. This would seem to reflect a greater concern in the retail sector for weeding out previously dishonest employees.

An examination of the three questions evaluating inventory control demonstrates a fair degree of consistency across the three industry sectors. There was consensus that the control of employee theft was considered a medium priority. This should not be taken to mean that employee theft was unimportant but that inventory-control personnel usually felt that theft prevention was a secondary objective when compared to their primary goal: assuring that sufficient inventory stock was available without tying up corporate assets by having too much material on hand. Some difference is evident concerning the executives' perceptions of how vulnerable inventory was to theft by employees. Retailers believed their inventory was most vulnerable; manufacturers felt their materials were least vulnerable. Finally, executives in all three sectors expressed satisfaction with the workings of inventory controls as they related to employee theft.

The last set of variables in table 8-3 focuses on security departments. Not surprisingly, retail firms had, on the average, the largest security departments. It is also instructive to examine the variance for this variable. Although hospitals and manufacturing firms had similar mean scores, considerably more variability was found in the size of security departments in manufacturing firms. In fact, of all the security staff employed in the manufacturing companies, over half work in one firm. (The reader should note that the ratio of security size/total organizational size is used in the upcoming analysis.)

The two indexes describing security departments demonstrate a similar pattern. Security departments within retail firms tended to be more sophisticated (that is, professional) and more oriented toward preventing employee theft than those departments in organizations from the other two sectors. Of these latter two sectors, hospitals tended to score higher on these indexes than manufacturers.

The information presented in table 8-4 provides a somewhat more-specific view of how organizations formally reacted against employee thieves. Before reviewing these data, however, two comments are in order. First, the readers should note that over one-third of the organizations possessed no records on dispositions of employee thieves. It is probable that organizations that apprehend and process large numbers of employee thieves are also likely to develop a bureaucracy to perform these actions, including the keeping of records. If this is true, then the organizations that do not keep official records of dispositions would tend to apprehend fewer thieves than these data suggest. Second, these data are based on official records compiled by security departments. They do not reflect cases of apprehended employees who are handled informally (that is, without contacting the security department).

Turning to the data in table 8-4, a clear pattern emerges. When compared to the other two sectors, retail firms apprehended more employees for stealing and penalized them more severely. Several additional observations might be made about disposition practices. First, a fairly obvious finding is that only a very small proportion of employees who steal is ever apprehended. Even for retail firms, which reported the highest level of apprehensions, the

Table 8-4
Descriptive Statistics: Organizational-Disposition Measures, by Sector

	Retail		Hospital		Manufacturing	
Measure	Mean	Standard Deviation	Mean	Standard Deviation	Mean	Standard Deviation
Number apprehended	91(10)[b]	49	7.2(10)	11.2	10.2(7)	22
Percent terminated[a]	98(10)	2	91 (7)	18	39 (5)	44
Percent prosecuted[a]	44(10)	30	16 (7)	21	25 (5)	43
Percent making restitution[a]	67(10)	23	0 (6)	0	2 (5)	4

[a]Percentage of those apprehended.

[b]Figures in parentheses refer to number of firms that possessed data on these variables.

average percentage who had been caught (5 percent of the work force) was relatively small when compared with the proportion of our respondents who admitted to theft (35 percent). While approximately 30 percent of those returning questionnaires in the hospital and manufacturing sectors claimed some involvement in theft, far less than 1 percent of the total work force was apprehended. Unfortunately, security records did not provide enough detail for us to assess how employee thieves who had been apprehended differed from those who were not.

A second finding derived from these data is that individuals who were apprehended for employee theft in at least two of the three industry sectors were almost certain to be terminated. An exception is found in manufacturing where less than half of apprehended workers were fired.

Considerably fewer cases of employee theft resulted in prosecution. Retail firms tended to prosecute the most frequently—about 40 percent of the time. Somewhat surprisingly, manufacturing firms, which were relatively lenient in terms of terminations, indicated a greater tendency to prosecute than hospitals.

The final type of penalty, restitution, was relatively common in retail firms where some form of financial restitution was required in two-thirds of the cases. In hospitals and manufacturing companies, restitution almost never occurred.

In conclusion, the disposition pattern disclosed here demonstrates some similarities with those uncovered in past research but also provides some new insights. The pattern we found in retail stores was fairly similar to the one uncovered in Gerald Robin's study of three retail department stores.[11] Both our study and his concluded that discharge is almost automatic for theft in retail whereas prosecution is less frequent. Our data may, however, indicate a change in the processing of employee theft. Offenders may be dealt with more harshly now than a decade ago. Robin's data indicate that, on the average, 17 percent of apprehended thieves were prosecuted and 45 percent made restitution.[12] Our study shows that 44 percent were prosecuted and that 67 percent made restitution. Our findings are more in line with prosecution rates reported in surveys by the Mass Retailing Institute and the National Retail Merchant's Association. They found prosecution rates of those apprehended in retail stores to be 31 percent and 39 percent respectively.[13] Finally, our data indicate that the pattern of theft disposition previously found in retail firms is not necessarily found in other industries. Hospital or manufacturing employees who steal tended to be treated less harshly than their counterparts in retail firms.

Controls and Organizational Rates of Property Deviance

The first set of zero-order correlations to be examined provides some brief descriptions concerning which types of organizations have the highest rate of theft. In table 8-5 we find information about the association between the size of an organization (measured in terms of number of employees) and its rate of theft. In two of the three industry sectors, hospitals and manufacturing, the relationship is positive, indicating that larger organizations have higher rates of theft. The relationship is, however, statistically significant only in hospitals. In retail firms the relationship is negative and not significant.

Additional descriptive data are provided in table 8-5, but only for hospitals. The reason for this limitation is that two of the measures, tax supported versus private and church affiliation, are clearly inappropriate for retail and manufacturing firms. The third, location, could not be determined readily for manufacturing and retail companies because they often have installations in many locations. Since each of the hospitals in the study is located at a single site, it is possible to give each hospital a score for this variable.

According to these data, the closer a hospital is to a downtown area, the higher its theft rate. Similarly, we find a fairly strong correlation between a hospital's being publicly owned (that is, tax supported) and its having a high theft rate. Federal, state, and county hospitals tend to have more theft involvement than privately owned hospitals. The third correlation demonstrates that hospitals affiliated with religious denominations tend to suffer less theft. This relationship is, however, neither particularly strong nor statistically significant.

Previously, we had hypothesized that higher levels of control would be related to lower rates of employee theft. The correlations in tables 8-6 and 8-7 specifically address those hypotheses. Looking first at the relationships described in table 8-6, several conclusions are immediately apparent. First,

Table 8-5
Pearson's Product-Moment Correlation: Demographic Measures with Organizational-Theft Rate, by Sector

	Organizational-Theft Rate		
Demographic Measures	Retail	Hospital	Manufacturing
Size	$-.24$	$.39^e$	$.31$
Location[a]	NA	$-.47^e$	NA
Public-Private[b]	NA	$.51^d$	NA
Church affiliated[c]	NA	$-.28$	NA

[a]Coded: 1 = Downtown, 2 = other urban, 3 = suburban.

[b]Coded: 1 − Tax supported (public), 0 = private.

[c]Coded: 1 = Church affiliated, 0 = non-church affiliated.

[d]Significant at .01.

[e]Significant at .05.

Table 8-6
Kendall's Rank-Order Correlation: Organizational Controls
with Organizational-Theft Rate, by Sector

| Controls | Organizational-Theft Rate | | |
	Retail	Hospital	Manufacturing
Policy	$-.62^a$	$-.18$	.09
Screening			
Performance	$-.24$	$-.51^a$	.32
Problems	.01	$-.04$	.19
Inventory			
Priority	.07	$-.23$	0
Vulnerability	$-.44^b$	$-.20$	.21
Satisfaction	$-.34^c$	$-.14$	.12
Security			
Size	$-.18$	$-.06$	.11
Sophistication	$-.27$	$-.17$	.12
Priority	$-.19$	.11	$.45^c$

Note: All variables are coded in such a way that a negative relationship is supportive of the hypothesis that higher control leads to lower theft.
[a]Significant at .001.
[b]Significant at .01.
[c]Significant at .05.

within each sector, the associations between the various controls and rates of theft are fairly consistent. Seven of the nine correlations in retail firms and eight of nine in hospitals are negative. Thus, for these two sectors, the relationships between control and theft rates are typically in the expected

Table 8-7
Pearson's Product-Moment Correlation: Disposition Measures
with Organizational-Theft Rate, by Sector

| Disposition Measures | Organizational-Theft Rate | | |
	Retail	Hospital	Manufacturing
Number apprehended	$-.54^a$	$-.43$	.56
Percent terminated[b]	$-.43$	$-.27$	$.87^a$
Percent prosecuted[b]	$-.08$	.53	.52
Percent making restitution[b]	$-.51$	c	.39

[a]Significant at .05
[b]Percent of those apprehended.
[c]No variance on variable.

(that is, negative) direction. Within the manufacturing sector, however, the relationships are uniformly positive.

Second, there is a fair degree of consistency between the retail and hospital sectors. For six of the nine independent variables, the correlations with employee theft hold across the two sectors. Again, manufacturing exhibits little similarity when compared to the other sectors. Third, if one examines the magnitude of these correlations, the conclusion is that controls tend to have a moderate to weak association with theft rates. Most of the coefficients are not strong enough to attain the .05 level of significance. Some exceptions do exist, however. In retail, for example, we find a fairly strong correlation between policy and theft. In addition, two of the inventory-control variables are statistically significant. Within the hospital sector, checking on prior job performance has a fairly strong and significant relationship with rate of theft. Finally, for manufacturing firms we find a moderate to strong association between one of the security variables, theft priority, and rate of employee theft. However, the association is in the opposite direction than we had hypothesized.

Turning now to table 8-7, we see a somewhat similar pattern to that just encountered. The effect of punishment of theft rates was relatively consistent within sectors and between the retail and hospital sectors. For these sectors, the numbers of apprehensions and terminations were related to lower rates of employee theft. The effects of prosecution and restitution, however, were much less clear. One should recall when reading this that these latter two sanctions are much less common—especially in hospitals and manufacturing firms. Only three hospitals and two manufacturing companies prosecuted any employees for theft in the year before this research was conducted.

Summary

The specific hypothesis being tested in this chapter is that organizations with more-sophisticated controls would tend to experience lowered rates of theft. Although our data indicate some support for this contention, the results are, at best, mixed. Within two sectors, retail and hospitals, most coefficients conform to the hypothesized, inverse relationship. Of the twenty-five coefficients calculated in these two industry sectors, twenty-one are negative as expected. Thus, controls do seem to have an inhibitory effect on the amount of theft found in an organization. Having said this, however, it is important to add that the influence of controls in most cases is extremely weak. Only five of the associations are strong enough to meet acceptable levels of statistical significance. Furthermore, our confidence in the ability of controls to have a major impact on employee theft is further diminished by the results found in the manufacturing sector. Although this sector had the least variance, nevertheless, an opposite pattern emerges as all of the coefficients are positively related to theft rates.

Employee Views of Specific Controls

The preceding discussion suggests that the direct effect of organizational controls (as we have measured them) is neither uniform nor strong. To obtain some understanding as to why controls are not more effective, we asked employees to describe their perceptions of the various controls operating within the work environment. The following sections present some selected responses of typical employees who were interviewed in the face-to-face section of our data collection. (The reader should note that no comments will be presented on pre-employment screening because most workers had little knowledge of screening procedures.)

Policy

Our face-to-face interviews with employees shed some light on the reasons organizations are not particularly effective in communicating a concern for employee theft. The issue of theft by employees is a sensitive one in organizations and must be handled with some discretion. A concern for theft must be expressed without creating an atmosphere of distrust and paranoia. If an organization places too much stress on the topic, honest employees may feel unfairly suspected, resulting in lowered morale and higher turnover. One employee we interviewed recounted having been employed previously at such a work place:

> Before I came here I worked at a place that made electric fans over in St. Paul. I'm not kidding, they searched us every night when we left work. They searched our lunch boxes and our clothes for tools and those little motors. It used to piss me off. That's why I came here. I don't like being treated like a thief all the time. I heard [present employer] was pretty good about that type of thing. They seem to be more worried about tardiness and not showing up for work than anything else. I've worked for a couple [of] supervisors who were really strict on that stuff. My boss now could give a lick. Basically, he just wants the work to get done. It might be different in other areas [of the company]. I don't know. [Maintenance technician]

For most of the firms in our sample, especially in the hospital and manufacturing sectors, policies on theft tended to be understated, not overstated. Most employees told us that organizational expectancies with regard to property are not clearly expressed. For many organizations in our sample, the only attempt made by organizational officials to demonstrate a concern for theft occurs when an individual is initially hired. While this appears to have some impact, our interviews indicate that reliance only on an employee manual or an orientation program to convey this message is not very successful. Upon entering an organization, a new employee is inundated with information. Employees cope with this information overload by focusing on those topics that are either especially important for their day-to-day job performance or that are given considerable attention. For example, hospital employees recall their CPR (cardiopulmonary resuscitation) training and discussions of hospital fire procedures because these items are emphasized as being important for patient safety. Few hospital employees had a recollection of policies regarding theft—not a surprising finding since their coverage consists of a single line in an employee manual or a perfunctory remark made during a security director's orientation speech.

Given the primary goals of a hospital, such a disproportionate allocation of time is sensible in that hospitals are more interested in saving lives than stopping employee theft. Therefore, it is not surprising that organizational expectations regarding material are not always clear to employees after orientation.

In retail firms, protection of property is more directly related to the primary goal of the organization. Thus, treatment of employee theft is elevated in terms of priorities. Coverage of theft in orientation often receives considerable attention. Several of the retail firms require new employees to sign a policy statement acknowledging their awareness of rules concerning property and that violation of those rules may result in prosecution. At least one retail company in our study shows a film on employee theft to all incoming employees. It seems likely that such measures might impress upon employees that their new employer treats theft as important.

The manner in which formal organizational practices are presented to incoming manufacturing workers and the emphasis that is attached to these formal practices vary significantly depending on the new employee's occupational classification. Professional and technically skilled individuals tend to receive very little information about organizational rules, regulations, or security measures. Rather, emphasis is placed upon company benefits and promotional opportunities. Normally, if any policy instruction is given to incoming exempt workers, it is provided by the area supervisor to whom the employee is likely to be assigned. Even this practice appears to be somewhat uncommon, however, as most exempt employees that we interviewed suggested that information about behavioral standards was gained for the most part from co-workers and by trial and error.

In contrast to this rather loosely structured approach to organizational rules is the environment experienced by nonexempt employees in manufacturing firms. When persons destined for nonexempt classifications are processed for employment in these companies, they receive a rather formal introduction to the policies, procedures, and security practices relevant to their particular work area. For example, when an assembler is hired to work the line, he or she first meets with the personnel officer who goes over the rules and expectations one by one. Often the individual also will be briefed by a supervisor who will again cover the rules and mention any others that might be specific to the work area. In addition to this briefing, the new employee will receive a worker's manual that he or she is required to read.

In any of the three sectors, coverage during orientation of the topic of employee theft may send an initial signal to employees about an organization's policy stance. Whether employees maintain such an impression probably depends upon whether or not they observe policies being enforced. Thus, over a period of time they may form other views on organizational concern for theft depending on what they observe on a day-to-day basis. As we discuss in chapter 10, the meaning of policy in an organization is principally determined during the daily interaction among an employee, co-workers, and the immediate supervisor.

Inventory Control

During the course of the intensive interviews, we obtained some insights into the workings of the inventory- and financial-control systems.

In hospitals, our interviews revealed two main points about inventory. One concerns the seeming overabundance of materials in patient areas of the hospital work environment. The second point deals with an unintended ramification associated with the computerization of inventory-control systems. The concern for patient care has a definite effect on the inventory of materials. In strategic areas where patient welfare may depend on supplies being available at crucial times, staff cannot afford to deplete an area of essential items. Consequently, there is a tendency to overstock supplies rather than to risk running out. The concern for patient care therefore may be said to have a definite, although indirect, effect on promoting theft of materials in that, with such overstocking, personnel develop a lack of concern for the efficient use of property. Because of this mentality, waste and pilferage are more likely to occur, as the following interview excerpt indicates:

> What surprised me a lot is how available the syringes and needles are. . . . They would just be easy for anyone to take. . . . I think it'd be nice if those things were a little bit tighter controlled. . . . I don't know

how you'd stop people from taking surgery equipment. Because again, when you see it all laying out there and you see it in big numbers [quantities], it seems like it doesn't cost anything; it seems like it's just free in a way, and I don't know how you'd ever change that. [Intern]

The computerization of inventory systems may also influence how employees view inventory. On the one hand, employees reported that the new inventory systems have led to an overall tightening of controls on patient-care supplies. This is particularly noticeable in the area of controls over medications and patient-chargeable items on the wards. We were told that more emphasis currently is placed on accounting for items that are used. It is no longer just a question of taking something from stock. Rather, most items come complete with a charge slip that must be entered onto the patient's account. Missing charge slips are a source of consternation. Employees cited frequent examples where supervisors, ward clerks, or co-workers expressed a concern for knowing how particular items had been used. This was needed so that they could fulfill the obligation to charge it to some patient's bill and thus account for its use. In hospitals where higher concern is manifest, employees seem to be less involved in theft.

There is a disturbing side effect, however, to computerized inventory controls—namely, our impression that the use of such inventory systems strips an object of its monetary value. According to our interviewees, in the past they had entered the dollar value of items on patient charge sheets. Now the employee merely punches in a series of code numbers. The result is an environment wherein employees have little sense of the values of items used or of the total monetary costs involved in patient care.

> Maybe I'm off the subject, but when I started in hospital supply, it was much different than it is now, we had to make out charges ourselves. We had a big book with the prices, so I was very aware of what the prices were. Now it all goes into a computer and I don't think that many people really know how much things cost because it's all done by numbers. But all the time I was really surprised at how much things did cost, and so now everything's done so much by computer that people lose sight of this. They had a program recently, a fair with big display tables set up in the cafeteria, where the cost of things was emphasized. [Hospital employee]

Retail employees mentioned that theft of cash is more difficult if a store's inventory is monitored through the use of computerized cash registers:

> Stealing from the register is very hard because everything is computerized and you can't ring up a sale at less than the amount because it's all computerized—the amount and the merchandise number. If something is on sale, you have to ring in that and put in all these numbers and then put the difference of the prices in. So it's really hard, I think, to steal from the register. At least, I couldn't think of any way to steal from the register. It's much more complicated than a lot of places. [Sales clerk]

The perceived futility on the part of some employees about attempting to steal from the cash register is revealed by another sales clerk:

> One of the girls that got canned . . . didn't get canned for taking money. This young lady went over to the women's department (she had a girlfriend over there), and she bought a shirt for $2 . . . it was a $25 shirt. Well, I guess every night . . . [the people at the credit office] go through those readout tapes, you know. [Sales clerk]

Another clerk was more respectful of the capabilities of point-of-sale cash-register control systems in her store:

> You'd ring [the item] for something [the correct amount], tell [the customer] that it was so much [a different, larger amount], and they'd pay and you'd keep the extra. That's probably the only way you could steal through the register because you punch it right in, it goes right to the computer, right to that board, and right on to Chicago. [Sales clerk]

At one of the traditional soft spots of inventory control, the loading dock, a far less-glowing account of the inventory-control system was given:

> *If you're going to take something out of the store, would the dock be a good place to do it?*
>
> Probably. And inventory is really horse shit! They don't know what they got. That's why it'd be easy to take something. I mean, if you're taking a lot of one thing, they'd know, but if you took just one microwave or one weight set or something, no one would know. Inventory's just . . . well, in fact they'll call us up and ask us if we have something . . . you know, look in the stock room and see if we have any. They don't know. [Stock worker]

This employee's comments become even more impressive when we contrast them with a typical statement given by a manager of a store's inventory-control system, the controller of another major retail outlet:

> In this store, if somebody was to take a TV out of the stock room, he'd [the manager] know—only because we happen to have a darn good television and stereo manager who keeps a perpetual inventory on everything that he has, both down here and on the floor as his people sell it. Discipline them to checking off a list, and maybe three times a week he can come down here and count his stock and verify it with his records. If he's missing one, he'll go back and recheck his figures and his sales checks, and he'll either come to the conclusion that it was stolen, in which case he turns in a known theft for investigation, or that one of our people forgot to check it off. [Store controller]

Finally, in interviews with manufacturing employees we found a fair amount of agreement that effective inventory and distribution procedures have been designed but are often not implemented.

You've mentioned the theft of some pretty valuable items. Do you get a sense that there's much of a concern about that kind of thing here?

No, I don't get that feeling. And it's partly the way the organization propagates that type of thing: It's not my department; I'm not going to be concerned about it. Let me give you an example. An item came to me, or I should say a pack of items was shipped to me, by mistake. I can't tell you specifically what the items were, but I can tell you they were worth over $1,500. I easily could have taken them and sold them. There was absolutely no record that I had received the package. But I took the trouble to trace back who most likely would have been asking for those things. . . . Most departments won't do that. [Engineer]

Some workers argued that the effective monitoring of materials (and perhaps time as well) was simply not cost-efficient for these organizations. It may be that bureaucratic efforts to control the utilization of resources are more of a financial burden to the firms under study than the costs stemming from their misuse, given the rate of rule violation under rather simple controls.

Security

The intensive employee interviews demonstrate that worker perceptions of security varied both within and across sectors. In the hospital sector, the two hospitals studied during the face-to-face-interview phase differed considerably in terms of their security departments. In one of the hospitals, employees characterized security as being friendly protectors of the work environment. One of their primary tasks is fire safety. In addition, they patrol the parking ramps to prevent thefts from employee's cars and assaults on employees, escort nurses to their vehicles late at night when the evening shift changes, make rounds, assist employees with difficult patients or unruly visitors, and are usually on call to deal with any problem that may occur.

Some employees on the nursing floors at this hospital said that security was highly visible—officers made rounds throughout the hospital and were prompt in responding to calls for assistance. The phrase *I'd call security* provided some insight into how other employees perceive security officers' roles. Security responds as troubleshooters, problem solvers, and a reliable source of assistance. The following is typical of the kind of response one obtains to the question: What kinds of things does the security department do?

You mean in their job? They walk around a lot. Take care of calls like "There's a person here and he's making a commotion." Basically, I look at their job more as a protection of the hospital from outsiders rather than a protection of the hospital from the insiders. We jokingly tell them they're making the world safe for democracy. [Hospital employee]

At our second hospital, the picture of security is strikingly different. The majority of employees appeared to have an extremely poor image of their security guards:

> But their security guards are not the type of people that make you feel secure [laughter]. . . . They, you know, are people that can't get any other type of job, basically. And I'm sure they're very poorly paid. They're older, I mean they're not in the prime. You can't compare it to a policeman, a deputy sheriff, or that. [Registered nurse]

The reasons for the security guards' poor image are based partly on the employee's direct observations and partly on rumor. On probing, the following clerical informant indicated her unwillingness to let security guards accompany her out to her car:

> I know if you worked a night shift, I'm sure you'd see more of them and I think maybe they even, if you would ask them, would walk you out to your car. Things like that.
>
> *Would you want them to escort you?*
>
> Well, I don't know any of them personally, but from some of them I've seen, probably not. You know, I have at times wondered why an institution like that would hire those types of people.
>
> *Tell me what you mean by "those types of people."*
>
> Well, they certainly are not professional looking or acting, and they look like they're just off the streets.

Part of the poor image develops when all employees see the guards doing is sleeping on the job, sitting around in the cafeterias, or reading a book. Employees are vague concerning the duties of the hospital's security guards since they were rarely seen on the wards or in any other place except the front lobby.

> *What are they like?*
>
> I've never seen them doing anything but sit. . . . I think their job is to sit. I come in at the beginning of the shift—the guy's sitting there—I go out and he's in the same place. [Nursing assistant]

It is evident that guards in each hospital are viewed differently. We have one organization where security relates to employees as firefighters, where the relations between security and other employees are friendly, where security is protective of staff against outside intruders, and where emphasis on safety precautions far outweighs any emphasis on precautions against theft. In the second hospital, we have an ineffectual, low-qualified security service that is perceived as part of the problem. Despite these differences, there is no reason to believe that either security department has an effect on theft behavior. In neither hospital do we find the impression that security's goal is to apprehend employees who steal. For this reason, employees fail to support the notion that security has a depressing effect on pilferage by employees.

In manufacturing, a similar situation appears to exist. While employees reported an awareness of the existence of security in their firms, they believed that security has little influence on employee theft. The following two quotes illustrate employees' perceptions of the ineffectiveness of security:

> For some place that is spending millions and millions of dollars a year on research and development, that is recognized as the number-one company in the industry, I think we are horrendously sloppy in the area of security. If I wanted to, or if I were a person from outside the company, if I wanted to get in that plant and have access to top secret stuff going on, I could do it. Easy. Easy ways to get a badge from somebody. To walk in unchallenged. To walk right down into the engineering lab and photograph prints, take parts, and do whatever you want to do. [The system will] keep people from walking out with a wheelbarrow full of things, but in the area of micro-miniaturization, someone could easily walk out with thousands and thousands of dollars of electronic parts in their lunch pail, and nobody would ever know. [Department manager]

> *I noticed that you have security guards here.*
>
> Ah, security's nothing.
>
> *If you wanted to walk out with something, you could walk right by?*
>
> Sure. the security guards are . . . what do I want to say? A front. . . . They're just a showpiece. [Production supervisor]

The reason for this lack of impact once again centers on the low priority assigned to employee theft.

> [T]hese individuals [those in authority] apparently are more worried about what goes out the back door aboard a truck going to a customer than what's going out the side door where the employees go. However, slowly but surely, I think the company is going to end up looking at both doors, rather than just the one. [Production supervisor]

These impressions contrast considerably with those held by retail employees. Here workers viewed security as being more consciously directed at stopping employee theft. The following quote is illustrative:

> They [security] are in contact with the supervisors on how to prevent theft. We have a conversation about how to keep theft down in a department.

They watch for customers stealing and they watch for employees stealing. If my registers start varying where I don't balance out the way I'm supposed to, security will be notified and they will watch the department for a while to see if it's just carelessness on the sales clerk's part or somebody stealing. I've lost two employees to theft. I started noticing something, and I talked to my staff and then I talked to the security manager, and they waited and caught them. [Supervisor]

Retail security officers are much more likely to pursue actively the suspected perpetrators of internal theft. Sometimes this includes fairly involved methods, as evidenced by the following:

Well, sometimes the guards will bait you. They'll leave stuff out and wait for you to take it. There was the case where they had this really nice hunting knife, and they use the knives around the dock area to do the boxes and stuff, but they usually have a regular little orange handle with this blade sticking out and the blade chopped off. Well, this was a nice hunting knife. It was sitting out. They have these tube stations where you put the tube in and it goes through the thing, it's like at the bank. Well, at the tube station they left one of these knives out, and some guy saw one and it's been sitting there and it didn't seem for anybody. Apparently there was no packaging around it. If there wasn't any packaging around it I might think "Hey, like, this is company property." But this guy took it and the guards got him. Maybe they thought the guy was a suspicious character and they wanted to see just how suspicious he was so they did that. [Dock worker]

Another tactic for dealing with theft was described by a security manager:

Another honesty test we do is we'll put a check, let's say a $20 personal check, into the back of the register drawer. Along with that check, I'll put a $10 or $20 bill, depending on what they like to take. Some people like to take $20 at a time, some people take $10 at a time, or $5, or whatever, but generally what their pattern is. So along with that check at the back of the register, I'll put a $10 bill and record the serial numbers. When that employee I suspect is up there working, I'll be observing from a blind or somewhere and I'll have credit or another investigator call and say there's a check missing in register so-and-so, could you check it out. "Open up the drawer and look back there and see if it's back there." Here I'm presenting another opportunity for them. I know it sounds like entrapment, but it isn't. It's perfectly legal and I've prosecuted people on this. It just goes to show that anybody's capable of it. This person probably was good for $200 in cash and he was smart. OK, he'd just finished four years of school. I had him go back to the register. Sure enough, he looked, found the check along with the $10 bill. Immediately he looked around, took the ten, folded it up and put it in his pocket right away. This is my leverage. So we called him in. I interviewed him and all he'd admit to was stealing that $10 bill. That's all he'd admit to. He would not admit to the $120 that I had him charted out for that I know he'd stolen but I couldn't prove it. I didn't have him on tape. Another method we use is videotape recorder with a camera over the register so I can record stealing. I've caught nine people this way in automotive and over in paint. I've got them on tape. [Security manager]

As mentioned previously, such aggressiveness in theft prevention does seem to have ramifications for employee morale, as the following excerpt describes:

> The security system is very good, almost overbearing. One time I purchased a sheet and later on decided to buy a tablecloth. I kept the sheet in the linen closet for some time and later, when I tried to use it, found that the table-cloth didn't fit. So I took them both back to exchange them, I left them there without taking care of them, and later security called me into their office and grilled me on what I was doing with the merchandise. My husband wanted me to quit right then, that they were accusing me of taking the stuff. I was very upset about the way security handled that. [Sales clerk]

Punishment

Our face-to-face interviews also shed some light on how workers perceive the likelihood of apprehension and punishment. For example, most retail workers believed that theft will result in termination. The overall feeling concerning formal sanctions was expressed most succinctly by a dock worker who stated:

> My interpretation of anything having to do with theft from the store is, if you rob you're going to get caught. People get caught all the time. I've only seen it happen a few times and those people are all gone. [Dock worker]

A personnel manager told us the following when responding to a question about whether he had ever not fired someone:

> No, we terminated someone the other day for $6 worth of stolen cokes, or $2 worth of stolen lures from sporting goods, or $2,000 worth of cash. Once we do not terminate someone for whatever, then we set a precedent. [Personnel manager]

Employees base this opinion on what they have heard of past incidents of employees who have been caught stealing. A number of such stories were circulating among the work force.

> A couple of weeks ago three people were fired from the men's clothing department, and two other people had been fired for theft because they had . . . well, it was really stupid. It was one person's thing in men's clothing, but two others helped. They marked something down to 50¢, a really nice shirt. When they checked it at employee check, of course the security person goes through there and checks the receipts. She went to the department manager and she said, "No, that isn't right." So they got fired for that. [Sales clerk]

A very different picture emerges from our conversations with those employed in either hospitals or manufacturing firms. Accounts of apprehensions for theft were found less frequently and tended to deal with minor thefts. The penalties for these offenses tended to be less severe than those detailed by retail workers. For example, manufacturing workers caught stealing a roll of copper wire in one instance were warned informally that further theft would end in termination and in another case were suspended for three days without pay.

Conclusion

The data presented in this chapter provide both good and bad news for organizational managers who want to take actions to reduce employee theft. The good news is that employee theft does seem to be susceptible to control efforts. In both retail firms and hospitals, various controls were related consistently to lowered rates of theft by employees. This finding held true for corporate-theft policy, checks on previous work performance, inventory vulnerability, satisfaction with inventory controls, security size, security sophistication, along with apprehensions and terminations for theft. Our data also indicate, however, that the impact of organizational controls is neither uniform nor very strong. In sum, formal organizational controls do negatively influence theft prevalence, but these effects must be understood in combination with the other factors influencing this phenomenon.

Notes

1. A. Etzioni, "Social Control: Organizational Aspects," *International Encyclopedia of Social Science* 14 (1967):369-402; and Etzioni, *A Comparative Analysis of Complex Organizations*, rev. ed. (New York: Free Press, 1975).

2. Max Weber, *The Theory of Social and Economic Organization*, trans. A.M. Henderson and T. Parsons (New York: Free Press, 1947).

3. J. Baum, "Effectiveness of an Attendance Control Policy in Reducing Chronic Absenteeism," *Personnel Psychology* 31 (1978):71-81; and Baum and S.A. Youngblood, "Impact of an Organizational Control Policy on Absenteeism, Performance, and Satisfaction," *Journal of Applied Psychology* 60 (1975):688-694.

4. Alvin W. Gouldner, *Wildcat Strike: A Study in Worker-Management Relationships* (New York: Harper & Row, 1954).

5. Donald N.M. Horning, "Blue Collar Theft: Conceptions of Property, Attitudes toward Pilfering, and Work Group Norms in a Modern Indus-

trial Plant," in *Crimes against Bureaucracy*, ed. Erwin O. Smigel and H. Laurence Ross (New York: Van Nostrand Reinhold, 1970), pp. 46-64.

6. A. Etzioni, "Organizational Control and Structure," in *Handbook of Organizations*, ed. James March (Chicago: Rand McNally, 1965), pp. 650-677.

7. J.P. Gibbs, "Crime, Punishment, and Deterrence," *Social Science Quarterly* 48 (1968):515-530; W.C. Bailey and R.W. Smith, "Punishment: Its Severity and Certainty," *Journal of Criminal Law, Criminology, and Police Science* 63 (1972):530-539; and C. Tittle and A. Rowe, "Moral Appeal, Sanction Threat, and Deviance: An Experimental Test," *Social Problems* 20 (1974):488-498.

8. G. Antunes and A.L. Hunt, "The Impact of Certainty and Severity of Punishment on Levels of Crime in American States: An Extended Analysis," *Journal of Criminal Law and Criminology* 64 (1973):486-493; and C.R. Tittle and C.H. Logan, "Sanctions and Deviance: Evidence and Remaining Questions," *Law and Society Review* 7 (1973):371-392.

9. G. Robin, "The Corporate and Judicial Disposition of Employee Thieves," in *Crimes against Bureaucracy*, eds. Erwin O. Smigel and H. Laurence Ross (New York: Van Nostrand Reinhold, 1970), pp. 119-142.

10. W.S. Robinson, "Ecological Correlations and the Behavior of Individuals," *American Sociological Review* 15 (1950):351-357.

11. Robin, "Corporate and Judicial Disposition."

12. Ibid.

13. National Mass Retailing Institute, *Store Thieves and Their Impact* (New York, 1973); and National Retail Merchants Association, *Crime against General Merchandise Department and Specialty Stores* (New York, 1975).

9 Employee Perceptions of Theft Controls

In the preceding chapter we documented a rather weak but consistent set of effects of the organization's control apparatus on rates of employee theft. This aggregate-level analysis raises some significant questions concerning the salience of the various control mechanisms available to management in shaping the behavior of its employees.

For example, if organizational controls are to act as a deterrent to property and production deviance, one would expect that they do so through an intervening variable—namely, the employee's perception of the risks (or certainty) of detection of his or her theft behavior. We hypothesize that organizational controls operate through the following social-psychological process: Increased controls heighten the perceptions of detection certainty that should thus decrease the propensity for property-theft involvement.

Certainty of Detection

As a first step in evaluating the effect of controls on employee behavior, we attempted to determine whether or not the employees in the self-report survey perceived any substantial risks for taking company property. Specifically, we asked each respondent to indicate his degree of agreement (very true to not at all true) with each of the following statements:

I believe I would be caught if I took something belonging to my employer.

My employer knows when people take company property.

Employees here are often checked on for violation of company rules and regulations.

There are some things at work that no one would care if I took.

Responses to these statements were summed to form an index that we called certainty of detection. (The Cronbach's Alpha for this index was .690.)

When we correlated employees' responses to our certainty-of-detection index with self-reported levels of property theft, we discovered substantial support for our hypothesis that perceptions of being detected are related to theft. If we examine the coefficients in table 9-1, we find that perceived cer-

Table 9-1
Pearson's Product-Moment Correlation: Perceived Certainty of Detection with Self-Reported Property-Deviance Involvement, by Sector

	Property Deviance		
	Retail	Hospitals	Manufacturing
Certainty of Detection	$-.29^a$	$-.29^a$	$-.24^a$

[a]Significant at $p \leq .001$

tainty of detection is inversely related to employee theft for respondents in all three industry sectors—that is, the stronger the perception that theft would be detected, the less the likelihood that the employee would engage in deviant behavior. With the possible of exception of the age variable (discussed in chapter 5), these coefficients are some of the strongest discovered during the entire study.

In sum, employees who believe that they would be caught are less likely to steal from their organizations. However, the strength and consistency of this relationship, when compared to the findings of the last chapter, are rather puzzling. While the perceived threat of punishment does seem to be working, the key question is who provides the social controls that constrain these forms of worker deviance?

Social Control in the Work Place

In order to understand the prevalence of property and production deviance, in this chapter we utilize a social-control model of behavior. In a social-control paradigm we are interested in the "social processes and structures tending to prevent and reduce deviance."[1] Two fundamental social-control processes are normally recognized. The first source of social control comes about through the internalization of group norms "wherein conformity to norms comes about through . . . socialization."[2] The other major social-control mechanism is "social reaction through external pressures in the form of sanctions from others."[3] Obviously, socialization processes are important in the formal work organization. However, employee behavior is most directly contrained by the second source of social control—namely, external pressures through both positive and negative sanctions.

Formal Social Controls

External social pressures toward conformity can be achieved through both formal and informal social controls. As we have seen in chapter 8, formal social controls are a product of the regularized bureaucratic rules and the corresponding sanctions established by those in power within the work organization (that is, management). Complex organizations rely upon formally instituted negative sanctions such as dismissal, demotion, and suspension both to encourage conformity with organizational behavior expectations and to single out deviant members of the work group.

Informal Social Controls

While formal social controls are no doubt important in shaping worker behavior, the available qualitative field research on employee deviance emphasizes the effect of informal work-group sanctions on this phenomenon. For example, Donald Horning's study of blue-collar theft in the manufacturing plant concluded that informal work-group norms regulated both the type and the amount of property theft.[4] In fact, the work group collectively defined the specific categories of property that could be taken by employees—namely, "property of uncertain ownership."[5] Horning concluded that employee pilferage was very much a group-supported activity even though the actual taking of property may occur alone or in secret.[6]

Other researchers studying entirely different employment settings also have observed the strong influence of the work group in regulating deviance and theft behavior among individual workers. Gerald Mars reports in his case study of dock workers that materials in shipment were taken according to the group-defined "value of the boat."[7] For theft to remain undetected by the authorities on the dock, articles in shipment had to be acquired with the active cooperation and approval of all members of the work group.[8] These studies and other like them seem to make the same point: that employee deviance is regulated by the informally established normative consensus of the work group.[9]

A related quantitative study conducted on the deterrent effect of sanction fear on criminal behavior by Charles Tittle is also of importance.[10] Although Tittle surveyed households, not work organizations, one of his instrument items focused on occupationally related "role specific deviance."[11] For those respondents currently employed in a formal organization, this item was operationalized as "making personal use of your employer's equipment."[12] These data clearly indicate that the loss of respect among one's acquaintances was the single most effective variable in predicting future deviant involvement.[13] Furthermore, Tittle's data also show that, in general, "the probability of suffering informal sanction is far more important than fear of formal sanctions" in deterring deviant activity.[13]

Two other studies that recently examined nonworker deviance—namely, shoplifting and marijuana use—also have concluded that informal sanctions by one's peers seem to be a stronger influence on deviant behavior than the threat of formal (that is, criminal/legal) sanctions.[14] Further, both studies seem to infer that informal sanctions operate independently of the presence of formal societal sanctions.

In summary, a review of the available literature allows us to hypothesize that the maintenance of social order in the formal work organization (as well as in society) will be far more dependent upon the nature of the reaction from one's co-workers than the more-formalized sanctions promulgated by either the company or the criminal-justice system. However, left unexamined is the possibility of an indirect effect of formal sanctions on the informal sanctioning process. Despite the preceding evidence to the contrary, there certainly must be some empirical evidence indicating the influence of formal sanctions on behavior, and if not, the direct impact of formal legal sanctions becomes questionable.

Our goal, then, is to compare empirically the relative salience of these two sources of external social control, formal and informal sanctions, in constraining deviant behavior by employees in a formal work organization. Specifically, we first examine the behavioral effect of perceived formal and informal sanctions on deviance commited by organization members. In addition, we assess the interrelationships between these two sources of social control constraining employee deviance. By comparing the direct and indirect effects of both formal and informal social controls, we hope better to assess the relative importance of each in understanding both deviant and conformist behavior within the formal work organization.

Operationalization

The measurement of the perceived severity of formal management sanctions was operationalized by asking each respondent to answer this question: For each of the following activities (the various property- and production-deviance items), what would be the most common reaction of persons in authority? The possible answer choices were (1) reward or promote, (2) do nothing, (3) reprimand or punish, (4) fire or dismiss, and (5) inform the police.

In order to measure the severity of informal co-worker sanctions for theft, we asked the respondent to answer the following question for each deviance item contained in the two dependent variables: What would be the most common reaction of your fellow workers? The possible response choices were (1) encourage, (2) do nothing, (3) discourage, (4) avoid the persons and (5) inform persons in authority. To maintain consistency with the operationalization of the dependent variables, for both our formal and informal measure we standardized the responses of each item and then summed across the group to achieve a single informal- and formal-sanction score for each respondent.

Analysis

Comparing the salience of perceived formal management sanctions to the perception of informal co-worker sanctions, both sources of social control were found to be correlated significantly to employee deviance in the predicted negative direction. As expected, employee perceptions of informal co-worker sanctions consistently demonstrated stronger negative coefficients than the threat of more-formalized sanctions promulgated by management.

Rather than a priori to assume there to be theoretical differences among the three industries, we tested for similarity of regression models for each industry sector by adding additional dummy-coded variables and their interaction terms into the original equation. Since the newly added terms reflecting industry did not explain significantly more variance than prior to their addition, data from the three sectors were combined into a single model. Even though slightly different items were used to measure property deviance in the three industries surveyed, collapsing across sectors was made possible by the standardization of the various items incorporated in the dependent variable. Since we found no significant difference in the regression coefficients for each of the three industry sectors surveyed, a single, composite model is presented in figures 9-1 and 9-2 for each type of employee deviance.

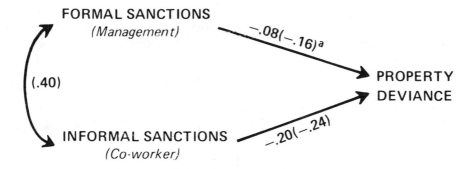

[a]Standardized Partial Regression Coefficients
(Zero-Order Correlation Coefficients in parentheses)

Figure 9-1. Perceived Social Controls and Property Deviance

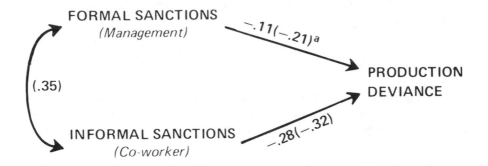

[a]Standardized Partial Regression Coefficients
(Zero-Order Correlation Coefficients in parentheses)

Figure 9-2. Perceived Social Controls and Production Deviance

By examining the configuration of variables in figures 9-1 and 9-2, we can appreciate the differential predictive salience of formal versus informal sources of social control. For both property and production deviance, the strength of the informal path coefficients are two and one-half times greater than the coefficients with formal sanction measures. Furthermore, when the standardized regression coefficients are compared to their respective zero-order correlations, we observe a substantial reduction in the strength of the relationship between formal sanctions and both property and production deviance, holding the effect of informal sanction constant. Thus, consistent with previous studies conducted in different social settings, employee behavior seems to be constrained more by the anticipated reaction to deviance by one's fellow co-workers than the threatened formal reaction on the part of management.

Since these results could be attributable to other temporally prior variables, it is important to test the stability of these relationships under control. Three demographic characteristics—age, gender, and marital status—factors that are usually recognized as important correlates of criminal behavior and delinquency, were chosen as controls. After dummy coding age (25 and under/over 25), gender (male/female), and marital status (married/unmarried), we included them as a group into the regression equations. As shown in table 9-2, both the standardized and unstandardized regression coefficients remain virtually unchanged despite the addition of these three control variables—themselves all independently related to employee deviance. Consequently, we may conclude that the relationship between formal- and informal-sanction threat and employee deviance persists independent of the employee's age, gender, and marital status.

Table 9-2
Standardized and Unstandardized Partial-Regression Coefficients with Property and Production Deviance, Including Controls

Independent Variable	Property Deviance				Production Deviance			
	Without Control		With Controls		Without Control		With Controls	
	Beta[a]	B[b]	Beta	B	Beta	B	Beta	B
Formal sanctions	− .08	− .08	− .08	− .08	− .11	− .10	− .10	− .10
Informal sanctions	− .20	− .17	− .16	− .13	− .28	− .25	− .22	− .20
Age	—	—	− .16	− .04	—	—	− .22	− .20
Gender	—	—	− .11	.78	—	—	.08	.54
Marital status	—	—	.06	.41	—	—	.07	.46
Intercept/ constant	—	.006	—	.95	—	.01	—	1.69
R^2	.06		.11		.12		.24	

[a]Standardized regression coefficient.
[b]Unstandardized regression coefficient.

Although we have thus far demonstrated the relative greater social-control salience of informal versus more-formalized management sanctions, the question still remains whether or not the threat of formal sanctions has any measurable effect on the prevalence of property and production employee deviance. It would seem that corporate policy regarding theft of property and time hypothetically should have some, albeit indirect, deterrent value. If we can assume that formal-sanction threats both predate and are perceived temporally prior to informal social controls, it may be possible to order causally our independent variables. We fully understand that this is a tenuous assumption given the perceptual quality of our two measures of the severity of social sanctions. However, threats of formal management sanction are normally presented to the neophyte worker during orientation programs prior to intensive interaction with one's day-to-day work group. Further, corporate policies specifying the response to deviance predate most employees' tenure with the company, especially in high-turnover industries like retailing and hospitals.

The decomposition analysis presented in table 9-3 clearly indicates that causal ordering does substantially clarify the nature of the independent-variable effects in our model. As predicted, formal sanctions do have an effect on the dependent variable, however indirectly through the perceived informal sanctions. Specifically, the indirect effects of formal sanction on employee deviance are − .08 and − .10 respectively for property and production deviance. Thus, if we accept the temporal-order argument, these

Table 9-3

Decomposition of the Effects of Formal- and Informal-Sanction Threat on Property and Production Deviance

Sanction Type	Total[a]	Direct[b]	Indirect[c]	Spurious[d]
Property deviance				
Formal sanctions	−.16	−.08	−.08	.00
Informal sanctions	−.24	−.20	—	−.04
Production deviance				
Formal sanctions	−.21	−.11	−.10	.00
Informal sanctions	−.32	−.28	—	−.04

[a]Zero-order correlation coefficients.
[b]Path coefficient.
[c]Impact of formal sanctions on dependent variable through informal sanctions.
[d]That part of the zero-order correlation attributable to common causes.

data also suggest that the perceptual severity of formalized sanction threats made by management do provide some social control of employee behavior, albeit indirectly, by shaping and reinforcing the prevailing worker normative structure in response to deviance by fellow employees.[15]

Conclusion

From these data we can appreciate better the relative social-control influences on work-place deviant behavior committed by employees. First, from our measure of detection certainty, we determined that employees are differentially involved in acts against the organization based, at least partially, upon their perceptions of getting caught. Further, these empirical results confirm findings suggested by earlier studies that imply that employee deviance is more constrained by informal social controls present in primary work-group relationships than by the more-formal reactions to deviance by those in positions of authority within the formal organization.

If an employee is not involved in deviant acts against the organization, that involvement may be deterred largely by the perception that fellow workers would not approve of his or her deviance. If formal management sanctions do have a social-control effect on deviance in the work place, they apparently operate indirectly by influencing the existing informal normative structure. Thus, policies and procedures unilaterally enacted by management no doubt will be ineffectual in constraining employee deviance unless they are also simultaneously reflected in the informal normative consensus of the work force.

Notes

1. Albert K. Cohen, *Deviance and Control* (Englewood Cliffs, N.J.: Prentice Hall, 1966), p. 39.

2. Marshall B. Clinard and Robert F. Meier, *Sociology of Deviant Behavior* 5th ed. (New York: Holt, Rinehart & Winston, 1979), p. 19.

3. Ibid.

4. D. Horning, "Blue Collar Theft: Conceptions of Property, Attitudes toward Pilfering, and Work Group Norms in a Modern Industrial Plant," in *Crimes against Bureaucracy,* eds. Erwin O. Smigel and H. Laurence Ross (New York: Van Nostrand Reinhold, 1970), pp. 46-64.

5. Ibid.

6. Ibid.

7. G. Mars, "Dock Pilferage: A Case Study in Occupational Theft," in *The Sociology of the Workplace,* ed. M. Warner (New York: Halsted Press, 1963), pp. 200-210.

8. Ibid.

9. Alvin Gouldner, *Wildcat Strike: A Study in Worker-Management Relationships* (New York: Harper & Row, 1954); J. Bensman and I. Gerver, "Crime and Punishment in the Factory: The Function of Deviancy in Maintaining the Social System," *American Sociological Review* 28 (1963): 588-598; D. Harper and F. Emmert, "Work Behavior in a Service Industry," *Social Forces* 42 (1963):216-225; and E. Stoddard, "The 'Informal Code' of Police Deviance: A Group Approach to 'Blue-Coat Crime'," *Journal of Criminal Law, Criminology and Police Science* 59 (1968):201-213.

10. C.R. Tittle, "Sanction Fear and the Maintenance of Social Order," *Social Forces* 55 (1977):579-596; and Tittle, *Sanctions and Social Deviance: The Question of Deterrence* (New York: Praeger, 1980).

11. Tittle, "Sanction Fear."

12. Tittle, *Sanctions and Social Deviance.*

13. Ibid.

14. Ibid.

15. R.E. Kraut, "Deterrent and Definitional Influences on Shoplifting," *Social Problems* 23 (1976):358-368; and L.S. Anderson, T.G. Chiricos, and G.P. Waldo, "Formal and Informal Sanctions: A Comparison of Deterrent Effects," *Social Problems* 25 (1977):103-114.

16. Excerpts from this analysis were taken from R.C. Hollinger and J.P. Clark, "Formal and Informal Social Controls of Employee Deviance," *The Sociological Quarterly* 23 (Summer 1982):333-343. Reprinted with permission.

10 Defining Property and Production Deviance in the Work Place

The vast majority of employee acts of taking company property or indulging in counterproductive behavior comes to no one's attention but the individual employee(s) directly involved. Beyond this, however, a large number of acts conceivably could come to the attention of co-workers, supervisors, security officers, or even the police; but of these, only a handful does. Two explanations are available to account for this selection process: (1) Operational definitions of property and production deviance, in fact, vary depending upon assessments of the situation by the specific participants, and (2) organizational-control mechanisms are limited in their abilities to prevent and respond to employee deviations. Based upon the findings of this book, we would suggest further that these two explanatory perspectives are closely related in that fluid definitions of deviance make organizational-control efforts problematic. These ineffective social-control performances contribute inordinately to unstable definitions of exactly what is deviant.

This chapter is focused upon an analysis of the social construction of deviance within the work place. We became interested in discovering the circumstances or processes under which certain acts come to be defined as deviant and thereby stimulate an organizational-control response. In the few previous studies of employee theft and other related instances of work-place deviance reviewed earlier, most authors have suggested significant situational determination of the definition of deviance and the quality of the reaction to it.[1] Current social theories of deviance are based upon the act's interpretation relative to the immediate social environs in which it is being defined, along with the possible conflicting deviance definitions that impinge upon the same behavior. There are no reasons why we would not expect this same general principle to operate within the corporate setting. In fact, other principles of formal organizations would suggest that the circumstances for unique and dynamic definitions of deviance inside modern corporate environments would be abundant.[2] The major theoretical and policy questions, then, are less of whether definitions of property and production deviance reflect the social dynamics of the organizational setting in which it occurs but more of how this influence is manifested and what are its consequences to our understanding of employee deviance.

Joe Raiche contributed significantly to the analysis and writing presented in this chapter.

Normative Incongruity and the Definitional Process

Even with our prior knowledge regarding the taking of property and related deviant acts by employees, we were impressed immediately with the extent to which, in practice, definitions of deviance were dominated by local work circumstances. At times, no specific norm or consistent rule seemed to exist to cover the situation. On other occasions, conflicting expectations existed and, in effect, freed employees to choose from among them or to reject them all. At yet other times, production-related priorities demanded modifications by supervisors of usual deviance definitions in order for employees to accomplish their basic occupational pursuits. The following excerpts illustrate the wide variation found in definitions of work-place deviance:

> We pass nourishments in the evening and we offer them [the patients] juices and pop and cookies and fruit, usually. We'll [employees] get fruit and crackers and cheese, and as long as they [the patients] get what they want I don't feel I'm stealing from patients. They get whatever they want and there's always enough left over. So that's why I feel comfortable doing this. [Hospital charge nurse]

> I do take sick leave when I'm not sick. I do sometimes take care of personal business on company time. I've also left work early a couple of times without my boss's say so and have made a few long-distance calls to my sister. But I think that's about the only things I've done. I wouldn't steal. [Manufacturing clerical worker]

Reproducible in many situations and with many different nuances, data like these make it evident that there is not uniform consensus among our interviewees on the way acceptable and nonacceptable behavior is defined. For example, it is apparently acceptable for workers in their unit to allow friends or relatives to benefit directly from the employee-discount privilege. This acceptability may be contingent on any number of factors—for example, the item is a gift, the department supervisor also does it all the time, the friend is poor, the employee involved in the transaction is a good, reliable worker, and so on. The point is that, regardless of the criteria of acceptability, the act of extending one's discount privilege to nonemployees is acceptable within this particular work group (which includes the supervisor) at this particular point in time. By recognizing that other departments and other work groups in this same retail department store have a different set of conditions for the acceptability of this act, or may even define this act as unacceptable under any circumstance, we begin to understand the essence of "normative incongruity."[3] We shall use this concept to mean the lack of consensus on standards of behavior within an organization due to the conflict among two or more norms, or the frequent shifting of normative expectations.

The concept of normative incongruity, however, does not suggest that the entire span of behaviors in a particular social unit like the aforementioned department store is without definitional convention. It may be that the circumstances for the proper use of the employee-discount privilege is, in fact, the only behavior in this organization about which there is a wide variety of practices. Rather, the condition of normative incongruity implies that a significant component of the behaviors in a given social context is without a uniformly agreed-upon normative standard. Hence, it is instructive to think of normative incongruity in terms of a continuum. There are, no doubt, degrees of normative clarity within every social unit. It is unlikely, however, that any social unit is completely without some degree of disagreement relative to the parameters of acceptable social conduct.

As part of our card-sort procedure (as described in chapter 2), employees for each of the three industry sectors were asked to discuss deviant events about which they had personal knowledge in their particular work areas. They were asked to articulate their views and, to the extent they could, those of their work mates of the behaviors identified. The following quotes are representative of employees' comments:

> You probably find that everybody in this plant takes stuff. And probably everybody in [the company] takes stuff. If you work in the electrical department and if you want a roll of tape, electricians don't buy tape, they just basically take it. He probably wants one roll of tape, fine. Who cares? Nobody really gives a damn. If you would take a box of switches, then it's something different. If you're going to set yourself up as an independent contractor in your spare time, on your own time, and so you're using the company, it's company material, that's when it gets serious. But nobody really cares if somebody maybe wants a plug, and a lot of the time the rule is you ask first. [Manufacuring electrician]

> Linen—people like bachelors and stuff don't like to pay a lot of money for that—I could see that. I've heard of people doing it. [Nursing assistant]

> Things like taking pencils and things home from the office: They'll never come out and tell you it's all right, but they expect it I'm sure. I know for a fact that they order extra, for what do you call it? "Company take home?" I think you'll find that anywhere. Things like this are not all that important. I'm not saying that it's what we should do; I'm just saying it goes on everywhere. [Manufacturing technician]

> On the floors [wards], people are more interested in things they feel are vital. They think that a patient's health and well-being are vital, and they can't attach too much importance to petty little materials things like using too much stuff or giving it away. I approve of the idea of having your priorities in order as far as people being more important. [Hospital central supply worker]

> For a lot of these things, you don't necessarily like the fact that it's going on, but it's the accepted thing. Well, maybe not accepted, but more people

do it than not. There are some things I can't see accepting, though. To me anything that's worth more than $10 in value is off limits. [Manufacturing production worker]

Any of these [property theft items] kind of depend. There are really unwritten limits on what you can and cannot walk off with, I guess. I see a certain amount of these types of things all over now, and I always have. It doesn't strike me as a real problem unless, obviously, somebody takes 100,000 boxes of paper clips or something. Something like that crosses over into the fuzzy area. [Manufacturing Supervisor]

From voluminous evidence of the type cited here, it is evident that work-place expectations and sanctions are permissive enough, in practice, to allow for a wide range and considerable volume of taking of company resources. These and other data from interviewees also reveal considerable variance in the standards against which workers judge the acceptability of many activities encountered in the organizational context. In all three industry sectors we found definitional inconsistencies within work groups, as well as between them, relative to activities discussed in the card sort. Not only did the definitional variations reflect the personal interpretations of the interviewee's own behaviors, but also they provided extensive information about the perspectives of work groups and employing organizations.

Noteworthy in the extended conversations with employees is that workers appear to be uncertain of formal organizational expectancies relative to most of the activities discussed. This ambiguity is illustrated by the fact that local norms specified by workers often set parameters for the degree of production time and property misuse that was acceptable in their work context, rather than whether the basic act was acceptable or not acceptable. The specified latitude that the local rules permitted varies greatly by work group and situation.

Testimony to the existence of a gray area within which acts can be labeled acceptable or deviant depending upon situational factors was enormous and persuasive. The gray area symbolizes the perceptual and behavioral implications of an inconsistent or unusually unclear normative environment. To employees, where certain behavior is neither clearly acceptable nor unacceptable, the gray area is enlarged and local situational determinants become more important to the definitional process. For example, the less employees can predict the reactions of their co-workers and/or supervisors to certain behavior, the more vulnerable they feel, the more unfair or capricious they view sanctions, and the more neglectful and incompetent they view management nonresponse. In this situation, most constraints on deviance are effected at the work-group level either by co-worker pressures or the supervisor on the basis of local legitimation, not of the organization. Thus, employees frequently must define what is acceptable or unacceptable from actions of the supervisor and conventional work-group practices that are subject to many production-related influences.

Normative incongruity emanates from a rather complex matrix of structural and interpretive factors in the work place that combine to provide definitional substance to the gamut of work-related behaviors pervasive in the organizational setting. An effort was made there to determine whether selected elements of the control structures evidenced within retail, hospital, and manufacturing organizations have an impact on employee-deviance levels in these settings. It was argued that the potential effects of the various control mechanisms were reduced significantly because of the organizations' failure either to communicate their expectancies effectively to workers or consistently to react to deviant behavior. As was implied in chapter 9, these patterns of organizational ineffectiveness are thought to play a significant role in shaping employee perceptions of the types of conduct that are acceptable in their particular work environments.

The behavioral definition of deviance, then, is a dynamic process involving both structural and interpretive factors. This process is one of definitional transformation wherein application of the label of unacceptable is given to an activity previously tolerated in the organizational setting and of definitional maintenance, reinforcing previously established labels of acceptable or nonacceptable. Rules of the work place not only are bent to fit the situation but also are constituted and reconstituted to reflect the compelling circumstances of the current situation that is dominated by production demands of the work organization.

Management of Deviance by Supervisors

In the realm of everyday life, it is commonly suggested that rules are made to be broken. In the work organizational setting, it might be accurate to amend this popular maxim to say that rules are made to be defined and applied locally. We gain considerable insight into the process of redefinition of acceptable and unacceptable behavior in the work context from the following quote:

> In a company of this size, of course, you [a supervisor] must have a certain degree of control over the way things are handled. There has to be a right and wrong way to do things. But you can't always go by the book. If a supervisor goes strictly by the book with his people, he won't last long with them. There has to be some give and take. You have to look at the situation sometimes and not just base your decision on what a policy manual says. This is where a supervisor's experience and judgment is so important. Situations are rarely as cut and dried as the manual would have it. At times, . . . especially when you're dealing with the people who work for you day in and day out, you have to go with your own judgment and experience—at the risk of blowing a policy. [Manufacturing administrator]

The contention of this manufacturing administrator is that there has to be some give and take between a supervisor and the workers he or she oversees if the department or work group is to operate effectively. The implication is that subordinates have some degree of influence over their superiors in setting parameters for work-related conduct. The work normative environment, then, appears to be a product of negotiation between supervisors and the co-worker group. We attempt to come to grips with the process of negotiating the definition of deviant behavior at the level of the work group by examining the roles that accompany the supervisory position in the organizations studied.

The Role of Supervisor

Departmental and work-group supervisors in the three industry sectors examined appear to have two (intendedly distinct) functions. The primary function of supervisory personnel in these organizations is to coordinate the efforts of a group of workers toward some end (or set of ends). We say that this is their primary task because it appears to be the principal basis upon which supervisors are evaluated in the three industry sectors.

The secondary function served by supervisors, and the one of most interest to us, is that of maintaining a sense of order in the production process—that is, policing company and work-group behavioral standards. Along with the role of coordinator, then, supervisors are conferred with the responsibility of protecting organizational interests. This task presumably is accomplished through a supervisor's attempts to insure that formally established organizational policies, practices, and expectancies are being observed.

As implementors of the desires and wishes of management, supervisors are entrusted with considerable power. We found that, in large measure, the source of power wielded by supervisors is not that they directly implement formal controls but that they have considerable latitude to interpret the controls. The power resident in the latitude of rule interpretation provides the foundation of behavioral control of the work group. Interpretation of formal organizational expectancies of the manner in which the employee discharges his or her role, in essence, becomes the vehicle through which the department supervisor ensures his or her success. Hence, the manner in which a supervisor chooses to implement organizational expectancies is a relatively reliable indicator of the priorities against which employee behavior will be viewed within that particular segment of the organization.

Hospitals and Manufacturing

In the manufacturing and hospital sectors, for example, supervisors clearly placed considerably more emphasis on the coordinating dimension of their job than on the policing aspect. It should not surprise us, then, that supervisors in the manufacturing sector, particularly those involved in the process of production, were usually more rigid in their interpretation of policies relevant to time misuse than property transgressions, the critical element of mass production. However, the production supervisor quoted in the following passage maintains that there must be a happy medium with rule interpretation:

> There's a happy medium with rules. Some [supervisors] are stricter than others on rules and things, but none that I've seen enforces all the rules all the time. You couldn't—even if you wanted to—and no one would. The people on the line would revolt. I've seen it happen with newer supervisors. They learn. The successful supervisor is one who can find a happy medium where all parties are satisfied. A supervisor who is overly strict usually loses rapport with his workers. When that happens, it's hard to get anything done. [Production supervisor]

A nursing assistant articulates an attitude relatively pervasive among supervisors in the hospital sector, particularly those overseeing workers who spend a major portion of their time with patients—namely, they prefer whenever possible to ease tensions rather than to run the risk of creating them within the work group.

> I think she [the supervisor] would be concerned about theft. I'm sure she would be concerned if there was an incident where someone was punched in who wasn't there, some gross violations of that nature. In terms of most other aspects [deviant behaviors], I think she just has some of the same attitudes as the others—that taking longer breaks or grabbing a few extra aspirins or taking some tongue blades home is within the norms. She's also good at working with the employees, and even if she felt this [stealing] was grossly in error, . . . in order to keep tranquility and good relationships in the department, she would let these things ride. "Ah, it's not that important! Getting people there on time and having them work well is more important." [Nursing assistant]

This type of orientation is reflective of the high priority given the quality of patient care in the hospital sector. In contrast, we discovered a qualitative difference among clerical and housekeeping supervisors who generally adopted a more authoritarian stance toward their employees and ran their departments like tight ships. These non-patient-care supervisors create more social distance and remain further apart from work-group tensions. They seem more likely to use formal policies to discipline employees than informal attempts to maintain group cohesiveness.

In sum, hospital interviewees suggested that less rigidity of formal control is exercised over employees involved in direct patient care than is the case for clerical and housekeeping workers. This difference in supervision illustrates the way in which different occupational groups interpret the primary goals of their respective departments. On the hospital ward, property or production deviance is sanctioned only if it negatively affects patients.

In contrast to the hospital sector, the manufacturing-sector interviewees indicated that the differences in the level of deviant behavior among occupational groups were related to the way in which supervisors handle exempt versus nonexempt employees. Exempt employees typically include those workers who are salaried and who receive incentive pay in some cases, special inducements (including paid vacations and trips), and comprehensive benefits. These workers are considered to be professionals or highly skilled technicians. Nonexempt workers tend to be semiskilled types including assemblers, technicians, and office personnel. The mobility opportunities for these workers are somewhat less fixed than for exempt workers, and nonexempt employees receive a benefit package that is less comprehensive.

Manufacturing employees suggested that individuals involved in creative activities (exempt employees) must have a work environment that is relatively free from constraint and specified routines since the flow of ideas, unlike the flow of products from a manufacturing process, cannot be regimented, as in the following:

> Engineers [are] people who use their minds to design. You can't say to them, "Okay, I want you to sit down and design this today—and get it done!" The creating mind doesn't work that way. It has to have room. A person like this might get a pattern going and may sit and work for fourteen hours while that pattern is still in their mind. Why restrict them to a 7:00 to 3:30 day? Let them put in their hours. Let them put it in somewhat at their leisure. I'm not saying a guy should come in for a few days and do a month's work and then take two weeks off. But, at varied times throughout the day, maybe the guy just can't think, maybe can't draw something. He has to get away from it. Go for a walk. Go to a bookstore. Just sit and read. Then he can get his concentration back and finish the job. [Production administrator]

In contrast, for the nonexempt employee it was argued that the mechanical aspects of the production process and the physical assemblage of materials requires a rigid, more-ordered format, as the following manager describes:

> If I have to ship 40 modules a day of variety A, I have to ship 2,000 of this [component] and 1,200 of this [component]. I have to structure through the factory, schedules, . . . day by day, person by person. Just trying to maintain control of those thousands of parts and that continual streaming and flowing in the factory is a very difficult task—but it has to happen. If it breaks down, we start coming apart at the ends. It's all a full process. Now

that means if we need three people running the machine to make that part on that day, they have to show up for work, they have to make the parts between the hours of 7:00 and 4:00 because three others are coming . . . to make parts between 4:00 and 9:00. It's a very disciplined system—it's just like milking cows, so certain things have to happen, events, at certain times. [Production manager]

From the interviewees we learned that, of the two categories of workers in manufacturing firms (exempt and nonexempt), supervisors gave more freedom to exempt employees and were less strict with them in the enforcement of rules. The manufacturing-sector interviews thus suggested that differences in the style of supervision of workers probably is related to the differential involvement of occupational categories in certain property and production deviance, including the theft that was reported in the employee survey.

These quotes and interpretations are indicative of the posture that characterized organizations in the hospital and manufacturing sectors relative to many types of employee deviance. In these contexts, as long as a given behavior was not perceived to be an obstacle to the organization's pursuit of its primary goals, even though the activity conventionally might be seen as deviant, it would likely be defined as acceptable.

Retail

A slightly different perspective on the role of supervisors is available from the retail sector. The primary goal of a supervisor in a retail store is to show a profit in his or her department. Success or failure in meeting that goal has a direct influence upon a supervisor's career since another important evaluation of a supervisor's job performance is based on the department's sales record and since many supervisors receive commissions based upon departmental sales.

Supervisors normally do not participate in the sale of merchandise to customers. Therefore, a supervisor depends upon the sales volume of his or her employees to maintain a profitable department. To achieve a high sales volume, supervisors concentrate on keeping productivity high among those they supervise. Analysis of data derived from interviews with retail employees indicates that behavior that is counterproductive to the organization may not be reacted to as such within the department if it contributes to productivity or at least does not hinder it. For example, the misuse of the discount privilege does not interfere with sales in a department or with the shrinkage calculation. Thus, we were left with the impression of trade-offs being made between employee deviance and sales. As along as these activities do not get out of hand, negative sanctions are avoided. As one employee stated, "As long as it's kept quiet, as long as it doesn't cause anybody any trouble, then it's all right."

However, supervisors in some retail stores tended to be somewhat less flexible in their interpretations of company policy, particularly when an activity involved the misuse of company property. We gain insight as to why this might be the case via the following quote:

> [Our supervisors are] all appraised on inventory shrinkage—it's a big portion of their appraisal. As a matter of fact, to be satisfactory they're not allowed to have any inventory shrinkage. They're actually supposed to gain inventory! We write off 2 percent of their sales every month to their departments, and at the end of the year we expect them to recover 70 percent of that. So we're telling them that they've got to operate on a shrinkage of less than 60 percent of a percent, which is unheard of. [Retail store controller]

Hence, evaluation of supervisors in the retail sector is, at least in part, based on their respective abilities to maximize profit through minimizing shrinkage—some of which is likely due to employee theft. This, perhaps, explains why retail supervisors were often more attentive to the manner in which their subordinates use company property than hospital or manufacturing supervisors.

Conclusion

It should be evident at this point that the goals and priorities established by management have a tremendous impact on the way work-related activities are viewed in the organizational setting. That supervisory personnel in the three industry sectors are expected to coordinate effectively a group of workers, while at the same time to assume the role of rule interpreter, enforcer, and even rule maker suggests the potential for conflict in roles.

Retail, hospital, and manufacturing supervisory personnel at all levels are burdened with the dual roles of coordinating as well as policing their subordinates—that is, the classic foreman dilemma of being both a representative of management and one of the group trying to get things done. At times, the mandate of coordination is in direct conflict with that of safeguarding organizational rules and regulations. To resolve this conflict, we have found that supervisors almost always will exercise discretion in their implementation of formal organizational measures in favor of maintaining an effective department or work group. This is done because effective coordination of basic work-group production is the criterion most salient to evaluations of their individual performance and that of their subordinates.

It is not clear that supervisors actively bargain with their employees. Rather, supervisors, particularly those with years of experience, seem to sense that the co-worker group operates more successfully in a flexible normative environment than in a situation requiring strict adherence to organizational policies and procedures. Hence, the negotiation of deviance at the level of the work group is a rather subtle, interactive process. In a sense, supervisors barter flexibility or permissiveness in the work environment in return for the ability to predict (or expect) cooperative responses when the need arises.

> Management types sit down and write the policy they think is necessary to accomplish the things they want to accomplish. As supervisors, we take what they've written and interpret it our own way. We can't treat people like robots: "You're a minute late; you will be written up for being a minute late"; or "You've been late three times. You're fired." We take their [management's] strict rules and plug them into our atmosphere in a way that we feel is right and that will get the job done. [Manufacturing production supervisor]

This process commonly appears to run throughout each of the work organizations interviewed. Thus, the dynamic definition of deviance was characterized by a process through which supervisors managed the inevitable conflicts between the work-place rules (including those about property and production deviance) and the day-to-day production requirements of the unit.

Notes

1. D.L. Altheide et al. "The Social Meanings of Employee Theft," in *Crime at the Top,* eds. John M. Johnson and Jack D. Douglas (Philadelphia: Lippincott, 1978), pp. 90-124; and Donald N.M. Horning, "Blue Collar Theft: Conceptions of Property, Attitudes toward Pilfering, and Work Group Norms in a Modern Industrial Plant," in *Crimes against Bureaucracy,* eds. Erwin O. Smigel and H. Laurence Ross (New York: Van Nostrand Reinhold, 1970), pp. 46-64.

2. E. Gross, "Organization Structure and Organizational Crime," in *White-Collar Crime: Theory and Research,* eds. G. Geis and E. Stotland (Beverly Hills: Sage, 1980), pp. 52-76; Melville Dalton, *Men Who Manage* (New York: Wiley, 1959); and Alvin W. Gouldner, *Patterns of Industrial Bureaucracy* (Glencoe, Ill.: Free Press, 1954).

3. R.C. Hollinger, "Normative Incongruity in the Formal Work Organization" (Paper presented at the Midwest Sociological Society Annual Meetings, 13-16 April 1977, Minneapolis, Minnesota).

11 Summary and Policy Recommendations

This book has outlined the major sets of variables that have been found to affect the phenomenon of theft and deviance by employees in their work organizations. This final chapter summarizes these findings in addition to providing some policy recommendations that may be inferred from these data.

Taking company property was reported by about one-third of employees in the three industry sectors surveyed: retail, hospital, and electronics manufacturing. Most of the theft reported, however, was not very serious and occurred rather infrequently. In fact, the modal employee did not report any property theft. Even though we recognize that our data are obviously conservative estimates, we nevertheless feel that this book seriously challenges those who declare that everybody is stealing. Neither the survey data nor the face-to-face interviews support these often heard pessimistic assessments regarding the prevalence of property theft by employees. From a policy standpoint, this is a most important finding. Substantially increasing the internal-security presence does not seem to be appropriate given the prevalence of the problem. In fact, doing so may make things worse.

It is important to understand that the theft of property represents a minority share of the employee deviance that was discovered in the work organization. A theoretical and statistical relationship was established between involvement in property theft and participating in a broad range of counterproductive behaviors that we call production deviance. From the employee interviews and those with management teams, we found persuasive evidence that the same circumstances that foster the taking of company property also are related to the more-common manifestations of production deviance such as slow or sloppy workmanship, sick-leave abuse, long coffee breaks, alcohol and drug use at work, and coming to work late and leaving early.

Perhaps we have limited for too long our view of employee deviance to the theft of tangible property and assets. Instead, the theft of property should be considered as the criminally illegal portion of a much broader continuum that includes all deviant acts occurring within the work organization. As such, we should not be surprised to observe a hydraulic effect whereby an enforced decrease in the opportunity for property theft might easily lead to an increased prevalence in other detrimental acts affecting the productivity of the organization but not its tangible property.

Counter to a great deal of the literature about employee theft, we found that both property theft and counterproductive behavior can be explained best by factors intrinsic, not extrinsic, to the work setting. Although external economic pressure may explain the relatively rare cash embezzlement, when we examined its effect on employee theft we could find no significant relationship. Further, when we compared two substantially different metropolitan areas, we found no significant difference in their rates of employee theft within two different industry sectors. Even though economic and broader societal variables may help to explain street crime, this book could find no corresponding utility/benefit from these variables in understanding employee theft. Continuing to search for scapegoat explanations external to the work organization simply confuses our understanding of this essentially work-place phenomenon.

More important to management interested in reducing employee theft and counterproductive behavior should be a sensitivity to the perceptions and attitudes of its work force and in the manner in which the organization is addressing its behavioral standards. Although the typical employee in each industry sector expressed general satisfaction with his or her job, the dissatisfied employee was found in the self-report survey and the face-to-face interviews to be more frequently involved in property and production deviance. Further, those employees who are looking for a new job were more involved in work-place theft and deviance. In sum, we found that employees who felt that their employers and supervisors were concerned genuinely with the workers' best interests reported the least theft and deviance. When employees felt exploited by the company or by their supervisors (who represent the company in the eyes of the employee), we were not surprised to find these workers more involved in acts against the organization as a mechanism to correct perceptions of inequity or injustice.

Of particular concern to managers should be the younger members of the work force who reported significantly more deviance than their older co-workers. Not only was their level of dissatisfaction higher, but also we observed that these employees were not much deterred by the typical corporate sanction of dismissal for employee-theft violations. Since the younger employees have much less to risk in terms of wages, status, seniority, pension, career, and so forth, they apparently are not nearly as threatened by the prospect of losing their jobs as their older peers. Since criminal sanctions are used rarely by companies to punish apprehended thieves, the loss of a job is but a temporary inconvenience.

Obviously, the younger employee is a necessary and desirable component of the work force. What is essential for companies to understand are the contradictory messages they are sending to the young worker by often failing to treat them as bona fide employees. Typically, organizations reserve most perquisites and fringe benefits for the more-tenured and older employees. As a technique for reducing theft and deviance in the work place, this policy may exacerbate the problem. These data suggest that deviance was less common among those employees who perceive a vested, personal interest in the financial success of the company. Thus, if the employee can internalize the harm or negative impact of the theft or deviant act, we should expect a greater reluctance to act in a manner detrimental to the organization.

To integrate better the younger (or part-time) employee into the company, even if only for a short period of time, might be quite cost-effective in reducing theft, counterproductive behavior, and even turnover. Providing these employees with fringe benefits such as earlier merit wage increases, sick leave, better-balanced work hours, increasingly greater supervisory responsibilities, educational scholarships, profit sharing, possibility of promotional and career opportunities should help to eradicate the underlying justification for deviance. Many younger employees expressed that they experienced no remorse or guilt for their deviance because they perceived their work situation as a mutually exploitive one. The company was seen as "ripping them off" and they were simply responding in kind.

Certain occupations within a corporation have higher rates of theft and production deviance. This appears to reflect the differential access to materials and knowledge to utilize them by personnel, different control environments imposed by the company, and the nature of the work to be performed. In general, the greater the access of those in certain occupations to company material, the less specific controls imposed upon them, and the less routinized the job performance, the greater the reported property and production deviance.

There is clearly a dilemma here for persons concerned about the security of company property in an organization. In short, one simply cannot nail everything down. Draconian security devices such as cameras, one-way glass, mirrors, and the like may be a deterrent to nonemployees and shoplifters, but when directed at employees they tend to convey a message of distrust. Our research suggests that social controls, not physical controls, are in the long run the best deterrents to theft and deviance in the organization.

Employee-questionnaire data revealed that the best single predictor of involvement in theft and production deviance is the employee's perceived chance of being detected. Using data from executive interviews from which we measured the quality of orgnizational controls, we found modest but rather consistent relationships between the quality of these controls and the rate of theft admitted by employees in the self-report portion of the study. However, employee-interview data revealed limited awareness of organizational controls.

This limited awareness of organizational controls on theft suggests that firms must pay greater attention to four aspects of policy development:

1. A clear policy regarding theft behavior by employees must be formulated by management. Companies cannot rely on the adequacy or appropriateness of prohibitions regarding theft in the general society to apply also in the work place.

2. These policies cannot sit on the shelf and collect dust if they are to have the intended deterrent effect. Policy must be disseminated continually to the work force. The typical fifteen minutes during new-employee orientation is not adequate. In fact, our data suggest that presentations about ethical standards are frequently overwhelmed in pre-employment orientation programs by more-immediate and task-related information. Education and training programs must reiterate continually that taking company property is theft and will be negatively sanctioned. The structure of company operating standards must also consistently reflect this policy.

3. More important, the policies must be utilized to sanction deviant workers when they are detected. The promulgation of false threats probably does more harm than saying nothing about the subject. Further, the policy must be applied to cases of employee theft at all occupational levels on an equal basis. If higher-status employees get differential treatment than lower-level employees, this will greatly erode the fairness necessary to deter theft.

4. There are two types of deterrence—specific and general. Privately sanctioning the specific acts of the apprehended deviant probably does little to deter the many others who presently may be stealing or are considering involvement. To obtain general deterrence, these specific sanctions should not occur in a vacuum. Announcing to the work force (without using names, of course) that a number of employees have been sanctioned for theft will allow the remainder of employees to calculate realistically the risks of getting caught for their deviance.

The vulnerability of a firm's inventory-control system also has an effect on an organization's rate of theft. The critical factor in its effectiveness seems related to how the employees perceive the system is being utilized by management. If employees are allowed to conclude that the inventory-control data are only being used to resupply expended items without accounting for the use of previous items, the climate is ripe for theft opportunity. Too many employees told us that the company does not care about its property for us to minimize the importance of feedback in an aggressive loss-control system.

Pre-employment screening by the personnel department also can have an effect on the rate of theft in an organization, particularly if primary attention is focused on the selection of new employees who have demonstrated in the past a strong allegiance to their employers. Given the serious difficulties and costs involved in assessing an applicant's propensity for future theft (via polygraph examinations, for instance), the primary objectives of pre-employment screening should be directed toward the selection of those applicants who best can appreciate and internalize the harm done to the organization from deviant acts. Additionally, an emphasis on checking past employment histories may communicate to the remainder of the work force that the company cares about the caliber of its employees.

Given the multitude of other non-employee-theft-related responsibilities, it is not surprising to us that industrial-security departments, like their police counterparts in the general society, cannot by themselves hope to eliminate employee deviance. We found that the most effective role of security in deterring theft by employees is in communicating the loss-prevention role that the other departments such as the executive staff, inventory control, finance, and personnel play in implementing the company's policy on theft activity. Those firms with least theft were characterized by a pervasive and consistent message from all departments within the organization that theft was not acceptable behavior. The companies experiencing the most theft were those who inadvertently signaled that they were concerned with neither their property nor the well-being of their employees.

Despite these formal actions of management to control the level of theft, our book indicates that informal social controls initiated by fellow co-workers, such as gossip, ridicule, and ostracism, are much more-effective sanctions. Formal sanctions instituted by management are still important, however, but only indirectly as they help to shape the possible responses from one's co-workers. Thus, involvement in property and production deviance is constrained largely by the anticipated reaction of one's co-workers, not management. From a policy standpoint, this finding implies that actions enacted unilaterally by management will be substantially less effective unless they are correspondingly accepted and integrated into the normative consensus of the various work groups within the organization.

The extent to which these informal social-control mechanisms are important became even clearer during the face-to-face employee interviews where we discovered than an exact definition of property and production deviance is being modified continually in the work place. Although there is some consensus among employees on the conventional content of violative behavior, the near universal absence of either specific organizational expectations or consistency of action fosters circumstances in which situational determinants prevail. As a consequence, involvement in various kinds of employee deviance is tacitly negotiated with supervisors who broker potential deviance as a management resource in pursuit of personal, work-group, or company interests. Inconsistent and nonexistent organization standards permit a large pool of behaviors to be defined situationally into and out of employee-deviance categories. Under these conditions, which vary by corporation and industry sector, formal control by management retreats in deference to ad hoc definition and control by supervisors and work groups.

In summary, perhaps the most important overall policy implication that can be drawn from this book is that theft and work place deviance are in large part a reflection of how management at all levels of the organization is perceived by the employee. Specifically, if the employee is permitted to conclude that his or her contribution to the work place is not appreciated or that the organization does not seem to care about the theft of its property, we expect to find greater involvement. In conclusion, a lowered prevalence of employee theft may be one valuable consequence of a management team that is responsive to the current perceptions, attitudes, and needs of its work force.

Index

Age: and job dissatisfaction, 84-86; and property deviance, 63-65. *See also* Young

"Bad apple" theory, 91

Card sort procedures, 27; items used, 46-47
Certainty of detection, 119-120. *See also* Deterrence
Cleveland (Ohio): economic characteristics, 58-59; selection characteristics, 19-20
Community pressures, 58-60
Controls: organizational, 89, 100-103. *See also* Social Control
Corporate crime, 2
Counterproductive behavior. *See* Production deviance
Crime, nonviolent larceny rates, 19
Crimes against business: cost of, 2-5; corporate reaction to, 4-5

Dallas-Fort Worth (Tex.): economic characteristics, 59-60; selection characteristics, 19-20
Definitions of deviance, 129-133
Deterrence, 9, 93-94, 120-121. *See also* Punishment
Deviance. *See* Employee deviance
Dissatisfaction: dimensions measured, 80; general measures, 80, 82; job, 8; literature review, 79; specific measures, 82-85; theoretical implications of, 85-86

Economic factors, 6-7; theory, 53-55
Education and career, concern about, 66
Employee deviance: definition of, 9-10; employee awareness of, 46-52, 131-132. *See also* Property deviance and Production deviance
Employee theft: definition of, 2; prevalence of, 2-6; theories of, 6-9. *See also* Property deviance

Financial concern, 56-58

Hiring, control through, 91-92. *See also* Screening
Hospitals: public versus private, 104; supervisors, 135-136; type studied-Phase I, 18; type studied-Phase II, 20

Income: personal, 53-55; adequacy, 55-56
Industry sectors studied, 17
Intergenerational integrity hypothesis, 64-65, 67
Interviews: executive, 16, 25; face-to-face, 16, 25-27
Inventory control, 92-93; extent by industry, 101; measurement, 95-96; perceptions of, 109-112; and theft, 104-106

Mailing procedures, 23-25
"Management" of deviance, 133-139. *See also* Supervisors
Manufacturing: corporation type studied, 18; supervisors, 134-135
Marital status, 67
Methodology, rationale, 15 17
Minneapolis-St. Paul (Minn.): selection characteristics, 17-18, 19, 21

Normative incongruity, 130-133

Occupational: crime, 2; titles and production deviance, 71-72; titles and property deviance, 70-71
Opportunity for employee theft, 7-8, 69-70, 72-77
Organizations: property-deviance rates, 98-100; size and theft, 103-104; statistical analysis of, 97-98
Orientation, pre-employment, 108-109

Parallel deviance, 86
Phase I, research design, 17-19
Phase II, research design, 19-21
Policy: control through, 90-91; extent by industry, 100; employee perceptions of, 107-109; measurement of, 94; recommendations, 141-146; and theft, 104-106

About the Authors

Richard C. Hollinger is an assistant professor of sociology at the University of Florida, Gainesville, where he also holds a joint appointment in the Criminal Justice Program. Professor Hollinger was at Purdue University and at the University of Minnesota where he and Professor John Clark were coprincipal investigators of a three-year National Institute of Justice-sponsored research project entitled "Theft by Employees in Work Organizations." Professor Hollinger completed his bachelor- and masters-degree work at the University of Georgia in 1973, where he was elected as a member of Phi Beta Kappa. He received the Ph.D. in sociology in 1979 from the University of Minnesota. Professor Hollinger's teaching and research is focused on criminality and deviance with particular interest in the subject of white-collar crime. His present research is an empirical examination into the factors which lead to involvement in deviance and crime by computer. His recent publications have appeared in journals such as *Work and Occupations, The Sociological Quarterly, Social Forces,* and *The Journal of Criminal Justice.*

John P. Clark is a professor in the department of sociology at the University of Minnesota, Minneapolis, where he has served as departmental chair and associate dean to the College of Liberal Arts. Professor Clark completed his education at The Ohio State University, receiving the B.A. in 1949, the M.S. in 1957, and the Ph.D. in sociology in 1960. Professor Clark has been involved in numerous empirical research projects, most recently as coprincipal investigator (with Richard Hollinger) of the National Institute of Justice study, "Theft by Employees in Work Organizations." Other research and teaching interests are social-control organizations, criminal and delinquent behavior, and the processes involved in the definition of social deviance. Professor Clark's scholarly publications have appeared in journals such as *American Sociological Review, American Journal of Sociology, Journal of Criminal Law, Criminology and Police Science, Social Forces, Work and Occupations,* and *The Sociological Quarterly.* In addition, he coauthored *Youth In Modern Society* with his wife, Shirley A. Clark.